GEOGRAPHY

LONGMAN
REFERENCE
GUIDES

Steve Milner

|||||||||||||||||||||||||||
KU-364-927

Longman

Longman Group UK Limited,
Longman House, Burnt Mill, Harlow,
Essex CM20 2JE, England
and Associated Companies throughout the world.

© Longman Group UK Limited 1990

First published 1990

British Library Cataloguing in Publication Data

Milner, Steven
   Geography. – (Longman GCSE reference guides).
   1. England. Secondary Schools. Curriculum subjects:
   Geography G.C.S.E. examinations. Techniques
   I. Title
   910′.76

   ISBN 0-582-05792-2

Designed and produced by the Pen & Ink Book Company Ltd,
Huntingdon, Cambridgeshire

Set in 9/10pt Century Old Style

Printed and bound in Great Britain

HOW TO USE THIS BOOK

Throughout your GCSE course you will be coming across terms, ideas and definitions that are unfamiliar to you. The Longman Reference Guides provide a quick, easy-to-use source of information, fact and opinion. Each main term is listed alphabetically and, where appropriate, cross-referenced to related terms.

- Where a term or phrase appears in **different type** you can look up a separate entry under that heading elsewhere in the book.
- Where a term or phrase appears in **different type** and is set between two arrowhead symbols ◄ ►, it is particularly recommended that you turn to the entry for that heading.

ACKNOWLEDGEMENTS

I wish to convey my appreciation to colleagues at the London and East Anglian Group for sharing with me their experiences of GCSE examining, and for their consent to publish examination materials. However, without the constant support and forbearance of my family, the toils of examining and writing would not be possible. This book is therefore dedicated to Phillipa, Shaun and Hannah.

ACCESSIBILITY

The best location for many activities is the most accessible one. Accessibility means the ease with which places can be reached. It measures the possibility of movement taking place: the greater the accessibility, the greater the movement. As is clear from advertising material, industries and local authorities put great emphasis on their degree of accessibility when recommending themselves.

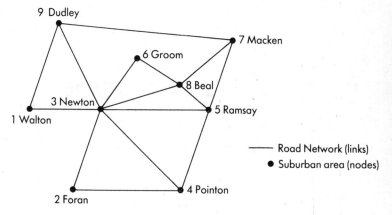

Fig. A.1 Topological map of an urban area

The most accessible location in an area can be determined. One way is to construct a shortest-path matrix from a **transport network** map of the area. As the example of an urban area given in Figs. A.1 and A.2 suggests, it is a question of counting the number of links between nodes. The lower the number of links, the greater the accessibility. The node with the lowest accessibility number is the most accessible place. In the example used here, that is Newton.

The problem with this approach to determining accessibility is that it does not consider important real-world factors such as **distance** and **population density**. Settlements with a large population will be more accessible to people

Surburban area	1	2	3	4	5	6	7	8	9	Total of links	Accessibility no.
1 Walton		2	1	2	2	2	2	2	1	14	2
2 Foran	2		1	2	2	2	3	2	2	16	3
3 Newton	1	1		1	1	1	2	1	1	9	2
4 Pointon	2	2	1		1	2	2	2	2	14	2
5 Ramsay	2	2	1	1		2	1	1	2	12	2
6 Groom	2	2	1	2	2		2	1	2	14	2
7 Macken	2	3	2	2	1	2		1	1	14	3
8 Beal	2	2	1	2	1	1	1		2	12	2
9 Dudley	1	2	1	2	2	2	1	2		13	2

N.B. Accessibility Number = number of links to reach the furthest node.

Fig. A.2 Shortest-path accessibility matrix

than smaller settlements. Considering distances and populations when deciding where to locate, say, a **superstore** or medical centre will minimise distances travelled and so find the most suitable and accessible location.

ACID RAIN

Acid rain is polluted rainfall, with a pH value of 5.6 or below. The pH scale measures the level of acidity of liquids, soil, etc. Rain with a high degree of acidity is considered to harm the environment. Across Europe, trees, especially conifers, are dying from the effects of acid rain. It is also thought to be responsible for slowly dissolving the external stonework of many historic buildings (e.g., Lincoln Cathedral, Westminster Abbey). Acid rain is produced by the burning of fossil fuels like coal and oil in power stations, and by the pollution from industry and road traffic. The emission of sulphur dioxide from coal-fired power stations is widely considered to be the main single cause of acid rain. Sulphur dioxide and various other chemical pollutants come back to the Earth's surface mixed with the rain.

In Britain, levels of acid rain tend to be higher on the east coast, with the rain less acid towards the west. Clean rain comes in with Atlantic westerly winds; 'dirty' rain comes from Europe, with its industry and population levels. Britain exports acid rain in the westerlies to Europe.

Manufacturing industry may bring benefits to many people in many countries but it has undesirable side effects like pollution. Atmospheric llution is a product of economic development in the developing countries the past two centuries. There is growing pressure to fit expensive equipment to power stations in order to reduce the emission of dioxide.

AGEING POPULATION

There have been significant changes in the age structure of the populations of most developed countries over the past twenty to thirty years. As a **population pyramid** for these countries, including Britain, would show, the average age of the population has increased over this period. There is a growing proportion of people aged over sixty; in the industrialised world as a whole this group accounts for about 20 per cent of the population and is growing. A combination of a small and falling birth rate and improving life expectancy is the cause. Fewer babies are born now than at times in the past and people are on average living longer.

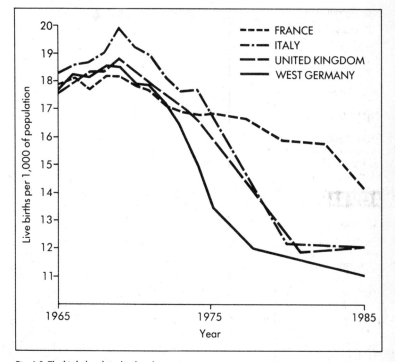

Fig. A.3 The birth dearth in developed countries

The declining birth rate in **developed countries** shown by the graph in Fig. A.3 is related to changing attitudes towards parenthood and the present availability and knowledge of the means to prevent births (contraception). The greater incidence of female employment has had a lowering effect on the birth rate. As living standards have risen, the birth rate has fallen, with children being seen as a financial liability and a constraint on living standards.

Improvements in **life expectancy** are due to better diet, medicine and general living conditions. People tend to live in better houses, eat more and better food and are served by better health care than in the past; consequently, the average length of life is longer.

An ageing population brings economic problems to a country. There will be a change in the pattern of demand for goods and services: e.g., the demand for wheelchairs, old peoples' homes, etc. will increase. The dependency ratio in the country will increase. This is the ratio between the productive population (people at work) and the non-productive population (e.g. children and senior citizens). In 1963 in Britain the ratio of workers to senior citizens was 5:1; in 1989 it was 3.7:1. It is expected to fall further in the future. The provision of pensions and medical care for the elderly may place a serious tax burden on the working population of the future.

AGGLOMERATION

Manufacturers concerned with similar types of work may come to similar decisions about where to locate their plant. Equally, manufacturers may consider closeness to factories producing component materials or similar products an important locational factor. Manufacturing firms and similar types of manufacturing work often group together in certain areas: e.g., at ports, at the site of raw materials and increasingly today in the main market regions close to customers. Regions and smaller areas specialise (as do countries and people) in producing those goods and services in which they have either a *comparative advantage* (they can produce better or cheaper than any other producer) or an *absolute advantage* (they can produce better or cheaper than any other area). This concentration of firms and specialisation of areas is known as industrial agglomeration or localisation; it occurs at both regional and local levels.

There are often clear economic benefits to a firm when it locates in a manufacturing area close to a number of other firms. External economies of scale (or economies that result from larger-scale production made possible by the local concentration of firms and shared by these firms) encourage the clustering together of manufacturers. External economies are of two main types:

- linked processes – e.g., the production process might be divided up, with individual plants specialising in a limited number of stages; there might be marketing links between firms, such as the sharing of a lorry's load;
- the local infrasturcture of services – e.g., the availability of services such as water supply, banking, transport, etc. and of a pool of skilled labour.

A localised industry is one which concentrates its firms in one area. The extent to which an industry is localised and a region specialised in their production can be measured using the following simple formula:

% of workers in the region employed in the industry
% of the country's workers employed in the industry

nber produced is known as the location quotient (LQ); it is useful for the distribution of industry. Light industry tends to be less localised vy industry and more widely dispersed. For instance, food, drink and tobacco manufacturing in Britain have regional LQs which range from 0.6 in Wales to 2.2 in East Anglia; metal manufacturing LQs range from 0.1 in East Anglia to 3.8 in Wales.

AGRI-BUSINESS

◀ Commercial farming ▶

AID

The USA has about a twentieth of the world's population and about a third of its wealth; China has about a quarter of the world's population and about a twentieth of its wealth. Foreign aid is a reaction to the enormous differences in **economic development** and wealth between the economically rich world and the economically poor world. Aid is development assistance, often in the form of money given by these rich countries to aid the economic development of the poor. Aid can be gifts or loans of money, the free help of advisers, gifts of technology, etc. Strictly speaking, it is a government affair and should be distinguished from emergency aid raised by private charities such as Oxfam, Band Aid, etc.

There are people who believe government foreign aid does more harm than good to the **developing countries**, especially if some is spent, say, on airlines and universities rather than roads and schools. Generally, people do agree that free trade with the developed world at fair prices is much more valuable to a developing country's economic progress than aid.

Fig. A.4 shows the breakdown of foreign aid given by various countries in 1985.

◀ International debt ▶

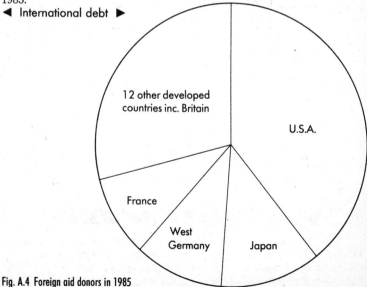

Fig. A.4 Foreign aid donors in 1985

AIR MASSES

These are large masses or air with uniform characteristics (temperature, humidity, etc.) carried with them from the place of origin. They are associated with the major winds. It is often said that 'winds bring the weather'; they certainly transport air from other places – places of origin and places on their route. For example, in winter cold air from polar regions (a polar continental air mass) can approach Britain as an easterly or north-easterly **wind**.

The importance of air masses in delivering 'Atlantic' or 'continental' weather to Britain is shown by Fig. A.5. Westerly air flows from the Atlantic tend to bring rain. Southerly and easterly winds tend to bring dry, continental weather. Our warmest weather is usually brought by southerly winds from the Mediterranean (a tropical continental air mass). The flow of air masses and wind direction are determined by the atmospheric pressure pattern.

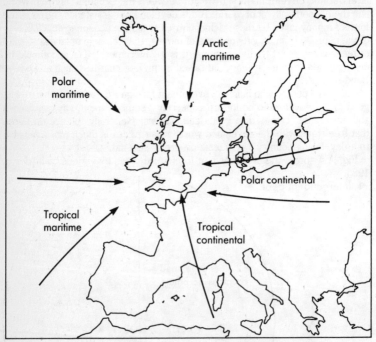

Fig. A.5 The major air masses influencing the climate of the British Isles

AIRPORT LOCATIONS

Siting an airport is an interesting decision-making exercise in which a range of sometimes conflicting factors has to be considered. Airports need:

- to be near/accessible to the centres of population (large towns and cities) they are intended to serve;

- a large area of flat, well-drained land at an economic price and capable of supporting concrete runways taking heavy aircraft;
- an area as free as possible from weather hazards, particularly fog;
- as few people as possible living along the flight paths.

The first and fourth points may conflict. It is difficult, perhaps impossible, to build an airport close to a large city without having a large population beneath flight paths.

Airport locations are often contentious, and opposition from some groups of people has to be considered both before the decision is taken and also during its operation. Farmers, industrialists and conservationists may oppose the use to which the land has been put; local residents are likely to resent the high noise levels.

Motorway links are generally important. They may reduce the scale of the local residents' opposition by enabling the airport to be located some distance from heavily populated areas.

City airports or STOLports (Short Take Off and Landing airports) are being developed in some cities (e.g., London City Airport, Docklands and Sheffield) to improve the speed of travel for business people. As Fig. G.11 shows, such airports are built inside the city and are therefore closer to business premises than major international airports. They are for short-haul flights (e.g., London–Brussels, London–Plymouth) and so use smaller aircraft, which need shorter runways.

ANTICYCLONES

Anticyclones are large, temporary areas of high atmospheric pressure, covering up to 2,000 miles. The isobars (lines joining places of equal pressure) form more or less concentric rings around the highest pressure (say, 1040 millibars) in the centre. Typically isobars are far apart in an anticyclone; calm weather and clear, cloudless skies are associated with an anticyclone. The air in an anticyclone is descending and is therefore warming and drying. After descending, the air circulates outwards in a clockwise direction in a Northern Hemisphere anticyclone. Winds in an anticyclone spiral out from the centre along the isobars.

Unlike **depressions**, anticyclones have no fronts, and they bring different weather conditions depending upon when they arrive. They are less frequent than depressions (about twelve a year over Britain as opposed to about forty depressions). They also move more slowly than depressions and so generally affect the weather for a longer period (seven to ten days). A situation known as a 'blocking high' can occur; an anticyclone becomes stationary, blocking the circulation for several weeks.

As anticyclones bring settled, stable, dry weather with little cloud at all times of the year, in summer this leads to 'heat waves'–hot, dry, sunny spells. In winter, however, anticyclones can lead to either clear, sunny spells or intensely cold, frosty and foggy spells, often referred to as 'anticyclonic gloom'. There is no cloud blanket at night to prevent radiation escaping into space. Fig. A.6 shows such winter weather conditions.

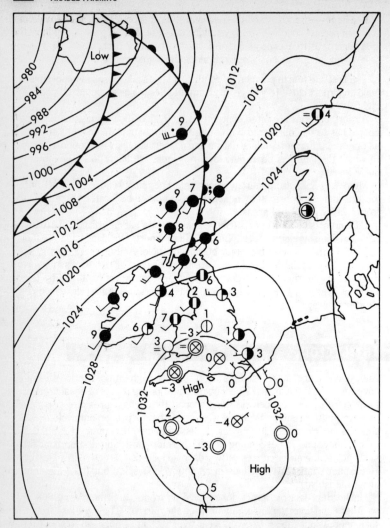

Fig. A.6 Weather map of British Isles and northern France showing 'anticyclonic gloom'

ARABLE FARMING

The Prairie Provinces of Canada have examples of arable farming. Farms tend to be large (about 800 hectares) and concentrate on crop growing (cereal or grain). The 194-hectare farm shown in Fig. A.7 is smaller than the average Prairie farm. Farming is extensive (i.e., large scale) but uses little human labour, partly because of the mechanised nature of the farming. The farm shown has two full-time workers and two part-time workers at harvest- and ploughing-time but five combine harvesters. Typically, Prairie farms use very advanced mechanisation and scientific farming techniques, including the computer analysis of soil fertility and crop spraying by helicopter. By general farming standards, yields per acre are, nevertheless, low. Prairie farms are commercial, selling most of the output outside the Prairie Provinces.

Many Prairie farms are diversifying their farming activities and are moving away from monoculture (e.g., wheat only, because wheat output has been rising faster than demand). The farm shown in Fig. A.7 grows a variety of cereal crops (wheat, oats and barley), flax for oilseed and has some pasture land for cattle.

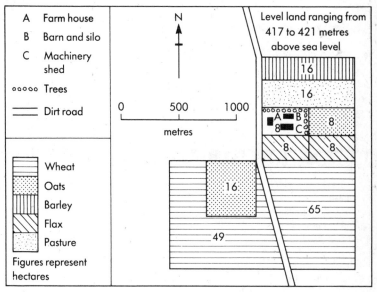

Fig. A.7 A Prairie farm

ASPECT

This refers to the direction in which a feature (slope, building, etc.) faces. It is of considerable local importance. Different aspects produce different micro-climates. The table shows winter temperatures on either side of a building.

South-facing wall	Time	North facing wall
5°C	8.00 a.m.	5°C
8°C	10.00 a.m.	6°C
10°C	12.00 noon	6°C
13°C	2.00 p.m.	6°C
12°C	4.00 p.m.	5°C
8°C	6.00 p.m.	4°C
6°C	8.00 p.m.	4°C
4°C	10.00 p.m.	4°C

The south-facing wall was nearly always significantly warmer.

Agriculturally, aspect is an important factor. The southerly aspect of the Swiss slopes around Lake Geneva results in greater vine and fruit production than on the north-facing French slopes (Fig. A.8).

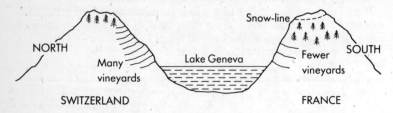

NORTH

Many vineyards

SWITZERLAND

Lake Geneva

Snow-line

Fewer vineyards

SOUTH

FRANCE

Fig. A.8 A comparison of the Swiss and French Alps

Aspect is crucial to the geography of many mountainous areas, particularly the Alpine valleys. The slopes with a northerly aspect are generally cooler, as they are often in shadow or out of the direct line of the sun's rays for a considerable part of the day.

ASSISTED AREAS

Since 1934 the British government has influenced the location of industry by attempting to encourage industry in those parts of the country known as 'Areas for Expansion' (Assisted Areas). This is part of the government's regional economic policy, which tries to ensure that there is a reasonable spread of economic activity across the country, and that employment and income are more equally shared out between the various regions. Regions in which there is a lack of industrial development, higher unemployment and lower wage rates can become named Areas for Expansion. In any industrialised or industrialising country, there will be regional economic differences occurring naturally, as some industries grow rapidly, others more slowly and still others actually decline.

The map in Fig. A.9 shows the location of the Assisted Areas split into Development Areas and Intermediate Areas. The Assisted Areas are either

- regions suffering from industrial depression because of the rundown of past industries – e.g., the heavy industries of North-East England, or
- regions with little industrial tradition – e.g., Cornwall.

They all have under-used resources, especially labour (i.e., high unemployment), which can damage community life.

At the same time, in the Standard Regions industry may be growing so that there is congestion, overcrowding and housing shortages, and perhaps a need to restrict the number of new factories being opened. Government policy has tried to take work to the workers in the Areas for Expansion rather than shift workers to the work in the Standard Regions.

Local authorities in the Areas for Expansion often place advertisements

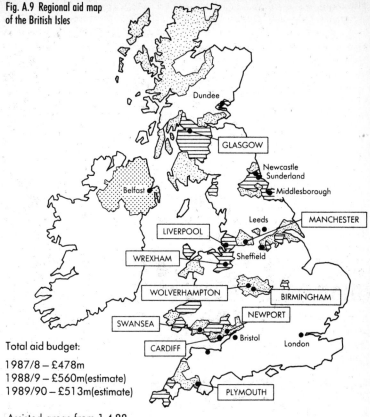

Fig. A.9 Regional aid map
of the British Isles

Total aid budget:

1987/8 – £478m
1988/9 – £560m(estimate)
1989/90 – £513m(estimate)

Assisted areas from 1.4.88

Development areas
New Regional Selective Assistance
New Investment Grants for firms employing fewer than 25 people
15% of capital expenditure (max. grant £15,000)
New innovation grants of 50% for firms employing fewer than 25 people
(max. grant £25,000)
New enterprise initiatives (govt. grant towards ⅔ of cost of
business consultancy schemes)

Intermediate areas
New regional selective assistance
New enterprise initiatives

Northern Ireland
Separately funded aid

Standard regions

designed to attract industry and stress their advantages over the Standard Regions, as well as government financial incentives. Grants from European Community funds have been made to the Areas for Expansion, often to improve their infrastructure for industry; e.g., the Keilder Reservoir project in Northumberland received £37 million from the European Regional Development Fund.

The task of encouraging manufacturers either to move to the Areas for Expansion from the Standard Regions or to open their new factories in the Areas for Expansion rather than in the Standard Regions is extremely difficult, but some firms have been willing to support the government's attempt.

The Areas for Expansion policy has been partly successful; it has slowed down the flood of firms setting up in the Standard Regions. Recent developments have been the introduction of Enterprise Zones and Urban Development Corporations in the London Docklands and Trafford Park, Manchester. Enterprise Zones have been successful in using government funds and attracting private money to support urban renewal and industrial development. (The Development Corporations in New Towns such as Milton Keynes, Crawley and Newton Aycliffe did a similar job of attracting industry at an earlier date).

Governments in many **developing countries** offer assistance to manufacturing industry as part of an attempt to develop the country economically: e.g., there are Government Industrial Estates in Kenya. Their actions may affect the location of industry, though policies of encouraging industrial development in specific regions are rare. The Brazilian government, for example, has attempted to spread industrial development away from the South and South East. Regional Development Agencies have been established. Tax incentives, loans and subsidies are available.

ATTITUDES

Modern geography studies places, people and current geographical issues in the world. Any investigation of current issues soon shows that people have different viewpoints (attitudes) about their causes, effects and any action that might need to be taken. For instance, **acid rain**, the **Channel Tunnel**, **deforestation**, excess farmland, **superstore** locations and **transnational companies** are all geographical issues about which people can be expected to express varying attitudes depending on their own personal values and beliefs. The same holds true for some of the key questions of geography: What is this place like? How is the place changing? What would it be like to live here? These questions are bound to lead to an expression of personal attitude and values. In answering them, justify opinions and judgements; always give reasons.

B

BETA INDEX

◀ Connectivity ▶

BIFURCATION RATIO

Stream order	Stream number	Bifurcation ratio
1	47	3.9
2	12	4
3	3	3
4	1	

NB: When counting the number of streams of a certain order, do not double count. There are only three places where second-order streams meet, hence three third-order streams.

There are 11 channel segments marked 3 on the map.

Fig. B.1 The River Kinder, Derbyshire: a fourth-order drainage basin

New Mills

One way of analysing the drainage system is to use Strahler's Stream-Ordering Technique. The earliest channels of a drainage basin near to its source are referred to as first-order channels. When two first-order channels join together, a second-order channel is formed, and so on. The drainage basin of the River Kinder is a fourth-order drainage basin; the river channel at New Mills has reached fourth order (Fig. B.1).

This drainage basin fits the Law of Stream Numbers, which states that there is an inverse relationship between stream order and stream number. The larger the order, the fewer the number, and vice versa. Comparing the total number of first-order channels in a drainage basin to the total number of second-order channels will give the bifurcation ratio. In the Kinder drainage basin the first- to second-order ratio is approximately 4 (47:12). An efficient drainage system will have a ratio of between 3 and 5.

BOULDER CLAY

Boulder clay or till is the material deposited by glaciers and ice sheets. Clay and stones are dragged along the base of moving ice and deposited at points where the ice melts, especially at the front edge and sides of a glacier or ice sheet. Plains can be covered in a thickness of boulder clay (e.g., East Anglia) or the boulder clay can be deposited as distinctly shaped features (e.g., drumlins).

Drumlins are elongated hills with their long axis pointing in the direction of the ice flow. They are normally 30–60 metres high, a third to half a mile long and are found in clusters, so producing a landscape commonly referred to as 'basket of eggs' topography. Examples can be found in North Lancashire and

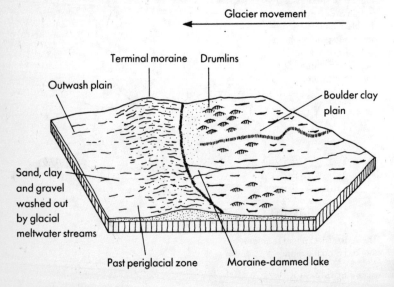

Fig. B.2 Glacial landscape

North Yorkshire, where the Lake District glaciers deposited boulder clay on this lower and more level land.

Moraines are ridges of boulder clay, though the term is often used to mean boulder clay or glacial till. Fig. B.2 shows a terminal moraine where the deposits have piled up at the snout of the glacier to form a ridge. Terminal moraines form at the terminus (end) of a glacier. The city of York stands on the Eskcrick terminal moraine, which marked the most southerly advance of one particular glaciation. Lateral moraines can line the edges of a moving glacier; they can often be found in upland valleys.

A terminal moraine marks the past border between a glacial and a periglacial area. Periglacial refers to the zone around the perimeter of the ice, an area not covered by it but none the less greatly affected by it. In northern latitudes at present this area is known as the tundra. At times during the Ice Age each part of Britain must have been periglaciated. This probably had a major impact on the nature of the British landscape we see today. Permafrost (ground permanently frozen at depth), solifluction (movement of soil downslope, perhaps during summer, when the top few inches of the normally frozen soil thaw and move over the permafrost below) and glacial meltwater from the melting, surrounding ice characterise the periglacial zone.

Boulder clay soils are agriculturally productive. The boulder clay plains of East Anglia and the North American Prairies are regions of productive cereal farming.

BRAIDING

Rivers and streams can develop a braided course. It occurs most commonly in the lower reaches of a river's course. From a single channel the river divides into a network of channels (Fig. B.3). The splitting-up of the river into various channels is thought to be the result of the large-scale deposition of sediment that occurs on a **flood plain**.

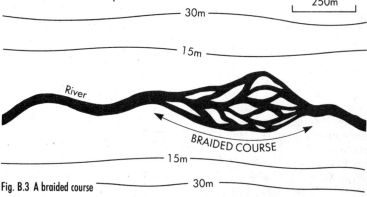

Fig. B.3 A braided course

BROWNFIELD SITE

◄ Greenfield site ►

CASH CROPPING

◀ Commercial farming ▶

CENTRAL BUSINESS DISTRICT (CBD)

The CBD of a large settlement (town or city) is its major shopping and commercial zone, offering the greatest range of goods and services in that settlement. The CBD is commonly referred to as the town or city centre; it will be the most accessible part of the town/city but is not necessarily the geometric centre of the settlement. Its location usually coincides with the original site of the settlement where it began centuries before (e.g., around a bridge). As the town grew and developed into a town, it spread away from this old core, which may have developed into the CBD.

CBDs are the main (highest-order) shopping centres in the town/city, containing the largest and most important shops (e.g., large department stores, chain stores, specialist shops such as menswear, the main specialist services e.g., the main post office, gas and electricity showrooms, and many of the settlement's office jobs. The zone serves the whole town/city and provides the greatest choice for shoppers in terms of both cost and quality as well as access to specialist services not found elsewhere. The larger the settlement, the greater the range and choice; city CBDs have a better choice and greater number of specialist goods and services than town CBDs. CBDs.

Bid-rents are at their highest in a town/city in the CBD, as Fig. C.1 shows. Land users will bid their highest price for land in the centre, with retailers making the highest bid. Roads, for instance, from all over the city meet in the centre; it is the focus of most transport routes and so the most accessible place for the greatest number of residents. As a result, land values are normally at their highest. More than other competing land users, retailers need maximum accessibility; they must attract large numbers of people. Large numbers of pedestrians during the day is a feature of CBDs; during the day they are the busiest place in the town/city. Most of these pedestrians tend not to live in the centre. The absence of residential population is another feature of most CBDs; most property developers have not bid as highly for the land as other potential users. The Barbican in central London is an exception.

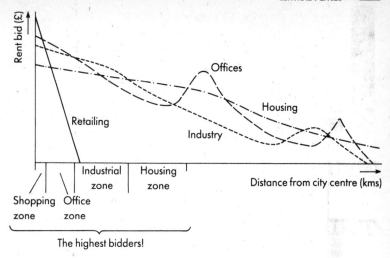

Fig. C.1 The rents that four users will pay for land at various places in a city

Other characteristics of CBDs – multi-storey buildings and a high intensity of building – result from the high value of CBD land. Tall buildings save on expensive land.

Certain functions provided by CBDs tend to cluster within parts of the zone. Shops selling 'shoppers' goods' tend to cluster so that customers may compare their goods (e.g., clothes and shoes). Certain professional services (e.g., legal and financial) tend to cluster so that business contact can be easier. The most profitable functions (e.g., large department stores) can afford the busiest, most accessible locations within the CBD.

In some cities geographers have recognised a core and a frame area within the CBD. In Nottingham the core area around the market square includes retailing (including the Victoria and Broadmarsh Shopping Centres), commercial offices, entertainment facilities and hotels. The frame area constitutes warehousing, small industrial premises, educational establishments, hospitals, government buildings and transport facilities (e.g., car parks). Traffic and pedestrian congestion can be a problem in CBDs. The presence of large car parks and the use of measures to relieve congestion (e.g., one-way systems) are a further feature of the modern CBD.

CENTRAL PLACES

In geography a central place is a settlement which has functions/services which make it a centre of attention for people from its surrounding area. Central places vary in importance; high-order centres, for instance, stock a wide variety of goods and services because they have the population needed to attract most functions (**threshold population**). People will be prepared to travel some distance for these functions. Ideas such as these have been used to try to explain the pattern of distribution of settlements: for instance, what processes are at work in the spacing of the large and smaller centres shown in Fig C.2.

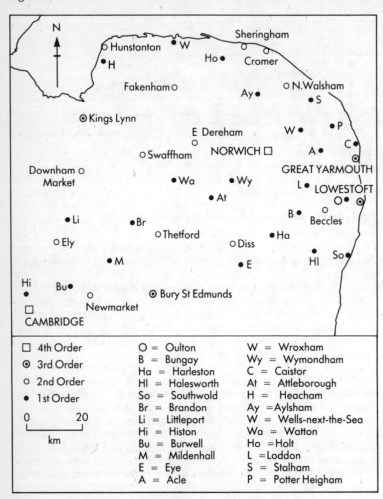

Fig C.2 Distribution of settlements in East Anglia

Central Place Theory is largely the work of a German geographer called Christaller, who was working in southern Germany in the 1930s, and it explains a regular distribution of settlement. Settlements have maximum spacing and are regularly distributed. Although larger urban settlements rarely seem to be nearer to each other than about 15 miles, random and clustered distributions are common because of the nature of a region's resources, transport facilities, etc. Fig. C.3 shows what these distributions look like on the ground.

	A random distribution
	A clustered distribution
	A regular distribution

Fig. C.3 Christaller's settlement distributions

Christaller explained regular distribution by suggesting that every central place develops around itself hexagonal spheres of influence (market areas); the size of the hexagon would depend on the order of the central place (size of the settlement). The overlapping hexagons shown in Fig. C.4 are for three settlements of differing size and importance. Each order of settlement – city, town, village – has a market area three times greater than the settlement below it in the hierarchy. Large city A's hexagonal area is three times larger than town B's, which in turn is three times larger than village C's.

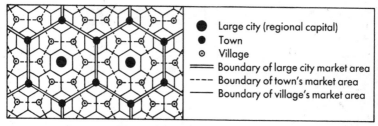

Fig. C.4 Christaller's overlapping hexagonal market area for settlements

Settlements are spaced at regular intervals so that market areas for similar-sized settlements are about the same size. A spatial arrangement of settlements that will enable these similar-sized market areas to be hexagonal will be the most efficient; circular market areas will leave some parts of the region either not covered or within two market areas. Real-world settlement patterns that might be explained by hexagonal market areas for settlements do exist. Careful study of settlement distribution is needed.

CHANNEL TUNNEL

The Franco-British Tunnel under the English Channel is due to be completed in 1993. It will provide a fixed link and so greater access to the rest of Europe for Britain (Fig. C.5). Drive-on/drive-off shuttle trains carrying cars and lorries, and high-speed trains will use the tunnel.

Business people and tourists are expected to benefit from the Tunnel but there is opposition from Kent residents, through whose county the increased traffic will be passing, and those people concerned that an influx of rabid animals and drugs might be made easier.

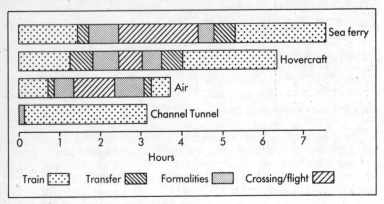

Fig. C.5 Comparative journey times: London to Paris

CHLOROPLETHS

Chloropleths are maps which use either colour-shading, line-shading or stippling to show a geographical distribution. They give average values per unit of area. For an example of a chloropleth, see Fig. D.8
◀ Isopleths ▶

CLIMATOGRAPH

This is a graph showing the monthly values for the two most significant aspects of a place's climate – temperature and **rainfall**. The twelve monthly temperatures are usually plotted as a line-graph and those for rainfall as vertical bars; both bars and the line are drawn on the same diagram. It is, therefore, possible to see clearly the main features of a place's climate: for example, its annual temperature range (the difference between the coldest and warmest months) and any seasonal distribution of rainfall. It must be remembered that the values plotted are climatic values; they are averages.

Fig. C.6 shows five climatographs, for Rio de Janeiro, Kano, Delhi, Kiev and Naples. Each represents a major type of climate to be found in the world. Climates are often classified according to whether they are Tropical, Temperate or Arctic (based on their latitude) and Continental or Oceanic (e.g., east coast or west coast). Note the importance of altitude (height) on a place's climate: Kano is wet by Tropical Savanna standards but it is 467 metres above sea level.

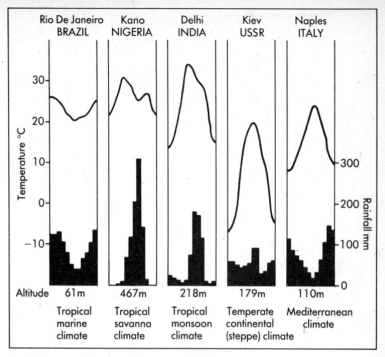

Fig. C.6 Climatographs for each of the major types of climate

CLOUDS

All clouds are the result of large-scale condensation taking place through a large volume of air. Such condensation is the result of prolonged cooling of the air. Air, which is forced to rise, expands because of the lower pressure it comes under, so it cools, with the result that its water vapour condenses into clouds. Condensation takes place when air is cooled below its dewpoint (the temperature at which water vapour condenses to minute droplets of water). Fog is cloud at ground level; the cooling and condensation occur at ground level rather than in the sky.

There are a number of different types of cloud and they are classified according to shape. Their shape depends on the way in which the cooling is brought about. The main types are shown in Fig. C.7 and each is associated with certain weather: for example, alto-cumulus with dry, warm summer weather; cumulo-nimbus with thunderstorms.

Cloud cover has both a reflective property on the sun's radiation and a blanketing property on the earth's radiation back to space. Clouds have a high albedo, that is, the ability to reflect radiation (white surfaces generally do

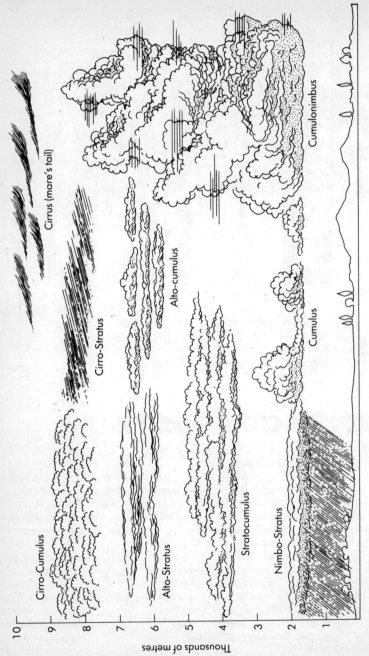

Fig. C.7 Types of cloud

have!). They help to prevent about half of the sun's radiation from reaching the earth's surface (Fig. C.8). The ability of clouds to act as a blanket can be seen most clearly in their absence; on clear nights with no cloud blanket to stop heat being radiated out into space, cold nights with possible dew, fog and frost can occur. Cloudy nights are usually warmer.

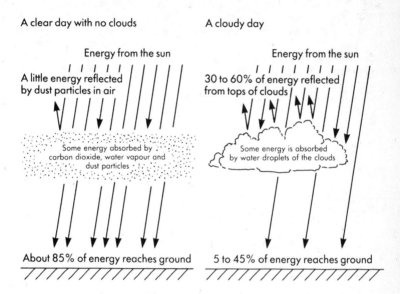

Fig. C.8 The effects of cloud cover

COLLECTIVE FARMING

In China, the USSR and Eastern European countries, farms are communally rather than privately owned. This grouping together under common ownership means that land, buildings, equipment, etc. are shared, farmers work together and profits are shared. Part of the profits go to the government.

On the whole, collective farms are a feature of centrally planned economies (communist societies), where the government controls the key parts of the economy, including food supply.

Collective farms tend to be large units run by a manager. China has about 50,000 farming communes, each typically 5,000 hectares with around 12,500 full-time farmers. The commune, though basically a very large collective farm, has non-agricultural features such as schools, clinics, communist party offices, etc. Each commune has a management committee of farmers and local people.

COMMERCIAL FARMING

Commercial farming is the growing of crops and/or rearing of livestock for sale rather than personal needs. Such production for the market is also known as cash cropping when it concerns the growing of crops; the term agri-business is also used. The extent of commercial farming in the world is shown in Fig. C.9. It exists in both the developed and developing worlds, but practically all farming in the **developed countries** is of a commercial nature, involving scientific practices such as the use of chemical fertilisers and advanced mechanisation, and in many cases production contracts with food-processing companies. The use of fertilisers and pesticides is considered harmful to human health and the environment by some people.

◄ Food supply, Subsistence farming ►

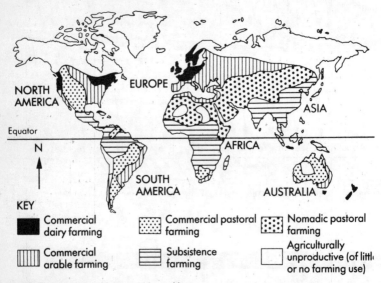

KEY

■ Commercial dairy farming

▥ Commercial arable farming

░ Commercial pastoral farming

⁙ Nomadic pastoral farming

▤ Subsistence farming

☐ Agriculturally unproductive (of little or no farming use)

Fig. C.9 The main types of farming in the world

COMMON AGRICULTURAL POLICY

The governments of many countries give help and support to farming, the most important of industries, and this can influence farmers' decisions. Without government interference farmers can never be sure how much money they will make. If, for instance, a farmer were to produce 400 pints of milk when the shops needed only 300 pints, then the price would drop so as to encourage people to buy extra and make sure that all the milk could be sold. If not enough milk were produced, then there would be a shortage in the shops and the price would rise. Prices could go up and down from year to year, and in bad farming years, when the weather was poor, some farmers might make very little money, and farmers not making enough money might stop producing food.

The twelve European Community countries work to a Common Agricultural Policy, developed to help their farming industries. This policy fixes the price of all farm produce regardless of whether there is too much or too little. The aim was to guarantee farmers a good price and a stable amount of money each year, and to keep prices for shoppers stable. Problems have appeared because the efficient farmers of Europe, using modern technology, have been able to increase production too much. All the overproduction that was not needed in the shops was bought up by the European Community, so that farmers could still get their money, and knowing this, farmers were encouraged to carry on producing extra. Before long huge stores of crops, meat and milk (the butter mountains, grain mountains, beef mountains and wine lakes) began to build up. The Community could not sell them and they were costing a fortune to store.

In the case of milk, storage was costing so much that dairy farmers were given a top limit which they could produce (known as a quota). Anyone going over the quota was fined. Milk production did fall but not by as much as was hoped. The problem was that sticking to the limits led to many marginal farms going bankrupt. This political decision in 1984 caused some farms in Britain to close down and others to change what they produced.

The Common Agricultural Policy also involves loans and grants of money being given to some farmers to enable them to buy new equipment, to encourage them to improve their land or to grow certain crops. The many fields of yellow oil-seed rape we see about us in Britain today are largely the result of the financial subsidies which that crop used to attract.

COMMUTING

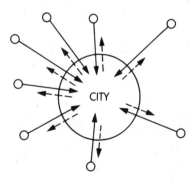

O Villages, inc. Dormitory
   settlements

◄━ ▬ ► Movements of people
   (daily journeys)

Fig. C.10 The daily movements of commuters

With the enormous improvement in transport facilities during this century has come the rise of commuting, that is, daily journeys to work of some distance and involving movement between two settlements. People travelling daily between their workplace in, say, London and their home in, say, Brighton, a journey of some 60 miles, are commuters. Fig. C.10 shows daily movements of commuters to and from a city.

The development of commuting has produced the dormitory settlement. Many of the towns in the London commuter belt, such as Reigate and Dorking in Surrey, are dormitory towns. These are largely residential towns where many people live but travel to other settlements for their work.

People often live some distance from their place of work for a variety of reasons. Modern transport facilities mean that they need no longer live where they work. Many choose to live in the more peaceful, open surroundings of the countryside. However, as you might expect, the friction of **distance** or the distance-decay model does apply to commuting; as Fig. C.11 shows the number of workers travelling to work in London declines as distance from the city increases.

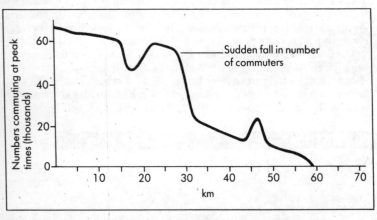

Fig. C.11 The numbers of people commuting to London along one main railway route

CONNECTIVITY

This is a measure of how 'connected up' a transport network is; in other words, of how easy it is to move from one node to another.

The most popular measure of connectivity used at GCSE is the so-called Beta Index, which is based on the relationship between the number of nodes and number of links in a transport network.

$$\text{Beta Index} = \frac{\text{number of links}}{\text{number of nodes}}$$

Generally speaking, Beta Index values below 1 indicate branching and disconnected networks (there are more nodes than links), whereas values above 1 indicate more connected, complex networks (the number of links exceeds the number of nodes).

Fig. C.12 shows *improving* connectivity, with the development of a transport network in a **developing country**, starting with the development of scattered seaports. Fig. C.13 shows *decreasing* connectivity in the reduction of the rail network in East Anglia during the present century. You will see that the Beta Index had grown to greater than 1 in coastal East Africa by 1985 and reduced to about 1 for railways in East Anglia by 1985. The connectivity of transport networks varies between countries.

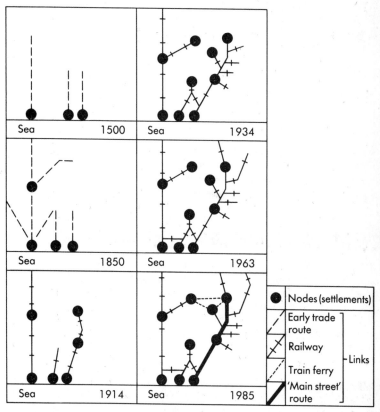

Fig. C.12 Improving connectivity: East African transport system

A positive correlation exists between the level of economic development of a country and the degree of connectivity of its railway networks. Developed countries tend to have well-connected rail networks; the overall network in some developing countries is less well connected.

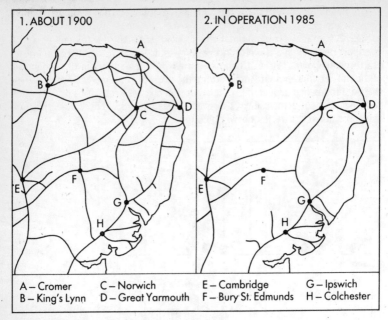

A – Cromer	C – Norwich
B – King's Lynn	D – Great Yarmouth

E – Cambridge	G – Ipswich
F – Bury St. Edmunds	H – Colchester

Fig. C.13 Decreasing connectivity: East Anglian railways

CONTINENTALITY

Distance from the sea has a massive impact on a place's climate. This is to do with the different rates at which land and water heat up and cool down. A body of water heats up far more slowly than a land surface. It takes about five times as much heat to raise the temperature of a given volume of water by 1°C as it does to raise the temperature of a similar volume of dry earth by the same amount. During the summer the land surface heats up quickly while the sun heats up slowly. During the winter the land surface cools very quickly, but the sea cools far more slowly and remains much warmer in comparison. The sea retains heat more effectively and tends in winter to heat up those areas of land which are close to it. Coastal areas tend to be warmed by the sea in winter and cooled by it in summer. The temperature range experienced by coastal areas tends to be quite small; this is the hallmark of an Oceanic or Maritime climate. The centres of large continents, however, because they are unaffected by the sea, tend to be hot in summer but very cold in winter. These extremes of temperature give a large temperature range which is the hallmark of a Continental climate. Continental climates have a greater seasonality of climate than do Oceanic climates; the seasons are more pronounced.
from the Atlantic increases; in other words, the summers become warmer, the winters colder and annual rainfall diminishes. The Atlantic is much warmer than the continent of Europe in winter, so winter westerly winds are relatively

warm. In summer the Atlantic westerly winds cool down Europe; the effect is more pronounced the further west you are.

This pattern can be seen in the east-west temperature profile across the Mediterranean Sea area. For example, Athens, Greece, and Malaga, Spain, have similar latitudes, 38° and 37°N. respectively, but there are interesting contrasts in their winter and summer temperatures and in their annual temperature range.

	Average January day temp. (°C)	Average July day temp. (°C)	Temperature range (°C)
Malaga, Spain	16	29	13
Athens, Greece	14	33	19

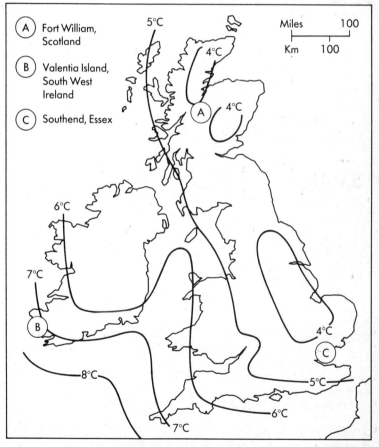

Fig. C.14 Winter sea level isotherms: mean temperatures for January

Malaga has a Mediterranean climate with a strong Atlantic influence. Athens's Mediterranean climate is more Continental, being hotter in summer but cooler in winter.

In the British Isles the most striking temperature differences are west–east rather than north–south. Figs. C.14 and C.15 do show that latitude is influential on summer temperatures but, more importantly, they indicate how temperatures change east–west/west–east along the same line of latitude during both seasons. The warmest temperatures are to be found in the west in winter but in the east in summer.

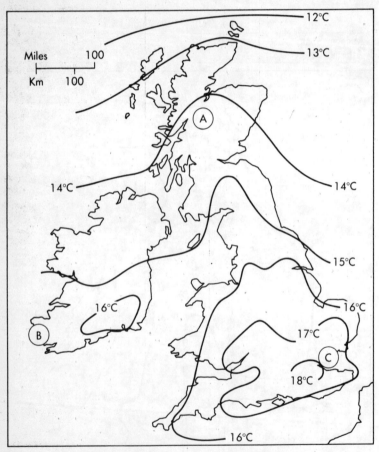

Fig. C.15 Summer sea level isotherms: mean temperatures for July

The factors determining the weather and climate of any locality include:
■ its position in relation to the **general circulation** of the atmosphere (the major wind belts of the world);

- the closeness to seas or large landmasses;
- its latitude (position relative to the Equator);
- local conditions such as altitude.

CONURBATION

A conurbation is a very large urban area formed by the joining together of several separate expanding towns/cities. Most of the 'green' land which formerly separated them becomes urbanised and a large, continuous, built-up area is produced. Conurbations normally have populations in excess of 1 million. They are the result of urban sprawl. Britain's seven conurbations–Greater London, the West Midlands, south-east Lancashire (Greater Manchester), Merseyside, West Yorkshire, Tyne and Wear, and Clydeside–together contain almost half the population of Britain.

Continued urbanisation in the world has seen not only the development of 'mega-cities', with populations of 10 million plus (e.g. Mexico City, Tokyo), but also super-conurbations (megalopolises). These are continuous, built-up areas covering very large areas and/or very large numbers of people; hundreds of square miles and perhaps 20 million people! Three examples occur in the USA: Boswash (*Bos*ton–New York–Philadelphia–Baltimore–*Wash*ington); Chipitts (*Chi*cago–Detroit–Cleveland–*Pitts*burgh); and Sansan (*San* Francisco–Los Angeles–*San* Diego). Conurbations have themselves coalesced into megalopolises. With continued suburbanisation of people and jobs, and long-distance **commuting** to work developing, will the Boswash megalopolis on the north-east seaboard and the Chipitts megalopolis around the Great Lakes one day coalesce?

CORRIE

◀ Glaciated upland ▶

CYCLONES

◀ Anticyclones, Depressions ▶

DEFORESTATION

The world's tropical rainforests are being cut and burned down at a rapid rate. Areas have been cleared of their trees throughout history, but the present rate is of particular concern. The rate of clearance of the 2 million square miles of Amazonian rainforest in Brazil is one of the most rapid. 10 per cent of the original Amazon rainforest has already gone, and at the current rate of clearance (1 acre per second) there will be no forest in Amazonia by the year 2010.

This deforestation is a major global problem which is not easily resolved because different people have different attitudes to the forest. There is a conflict of interest here, with two ways of seeing the Amazon rainforest.

First, there is the colonising/development view, openly represented by large landowners and cattle ranchers, who are eager to burn down the forest so that the land can be used for cattle pasture and the production of corned beef and hamburger exports. Brazilian governments have long dreamed of colonising Amazonia as a way of developing the country economically. They see a fully forested Amazonia as an obstacle to Brazilian economic progress, and wish that other people and countries would respect their need for economic progress and development. Amazonia covers half the area of Brazil.

Second, there is the save-the-forest view. This view is shared by the rubber-tappers, other rural workers and Amazonian Indians, whose livelihood and way of life depends on the forest, and by the developed countries of the world, with their ecological world standpoint. The rubber-tappers, rural workers and Amazonian Indians, whose activities have never, in the long-term, destroyed the forest environment, see deforestation as a threat to their way of life. The developed countries fear that deforestation could spell disaster for the world by enhancing the greenhouse effect. Burning the trees and their carbon will release more carbon dioxide in the atmosphere, and at the same time remove the 'lungs of the world'. Trees soak up the carbon dioxide released by industry and convert it into oxygen (i.e., they photosynthesise). Deforestation can cause world temperatures and sea levels to rise.

Deforestation can also cause flooding in another way. Fig. D.1 shows how deforestation in the foothills of the Himalayas in Nepal and Tibet helped to cause the Bangladeshi flood disaster in September 1988. 80 per cent of Bangladesh was under flood water from the rivers Ganges and Brahmaputra.

About 30 million people were made homeless. Population explosion in Nepal and Tibet, partly because of the control of malaria over the past thirty years has led to an increase in demand for fuel and new farmland on the slopes of the Himalayas. Consequently, on average, 120,000 acres of forest are cleared annually in Nepal.

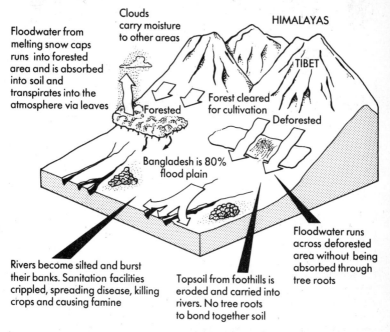

Fig. D.1 How cutting down trees in the Himalayas puts lives at risk

An international compromise needs to be worked out. The whole world not just the forested **developing countries** wanting to use the land for other purposes must pay the price of preserving the world's forests. One scheme is the 'Debt for Nature', whereby developed nations write off the debts owed to them by developing countries in return for the signing of commitments to preserve forests.

DELTA

This landform is built of river sediment (alluvium) at the mouth of a river. Deltas are most likely to occur where a river with a large load enters a sea or lake with weak tidal and current action. The river will deposit more sediment than the tides and currents can remove. Deltas are common in relatively tideless seas such as the Mediterranean (e.g., the Rhône delta, the Nile delta). Sea action does modify the size, shape and growth of a delta. Several types are recognised by geographers (Fig. D.2).

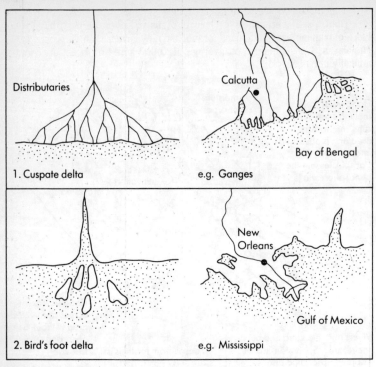

Fig. D.2 Two types of delta

DEPOSITION

This is a constructive landscape-forming process. Running water (rivers), ice, the sea, wind, etc. transport material which has been broken down. When this sediment is dropped and laid down, deposition is said to take place.

Examples of depositional landforms include flood plains due to river deposition; moraines due to glacial deposition; sand dunes due to wind deposition; spits and beaches due to deposition by the sea. Most new rock results from deposition: sediments deposited on the sea bed eventually form new sedimentary rocks such as sandstone, and the escape and laying down of hot lava from the molten interior of the Earth leads to the formation of igneous rocks such as basalt.

◀ Erosion, Weathering ▶

DEPRESSIONS

A temporary, moving cell of below average atmospheric pressure is known as a depression or cyclone. In the eye of the depression (its very centre) pressure can be around 970 millibars. Depressions are spawned or formed

Fig. D.3 The formation of a depression

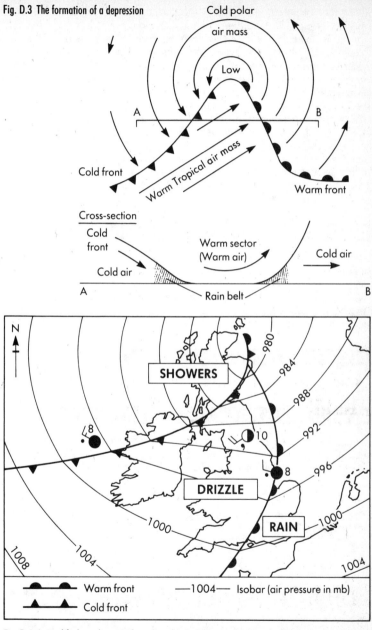

Fig. D.4 A simplified weather map for a day when a depression lay over the British Isles along the polar front in the mid-North Atlantic, where tropical and polar air masses interact. Within a depression these two types of air remain separate; the sloping boundary surfaces between them are called fronts (Fig. D.3). It is along the two fronts, the warm front and the cold front, that the weather changes; clouds and rainfall develop because the air of the warm sector is forced to rise and cool. The cold front advances more quickly than the warm front and eventually catches it up, resulting in all the warm air at the surface being replaced. This is known as the occlusion and is the start of the death, or filling-in, of the depression. It usually takes three to four days for formation to reach occlusion. During occlusion the depression becomes stationary; before, it was carried eastwards from the polar front by the prevailing westerly winds over the British Isles and spun anticlockwise in the process. A sequence of different weather conditions is experienced as the various parts of the depression pass overhead (Fig. D.4).

◀ Anticyclones ▶

DESALINATION

Building reservoirs is the normal means of providing water supply for people and industry. Removing the salt chemicals from sea water is a more expensive and less popular means, known as desalination. Desalination plants in the world are generally in developed countries who can afford the expense and technology more easily, and in or close to desert areas with their low rainfall and high demand for water.

DESIRE LINES

◀ Range ▶

DEVELOPED/DEVELOPING COUNTRIES

There is a wealth gap in the world, an ever-widening rift between the economically rich world and the economically poor world. Roughly 80 per cent of the world's population live in the so-called South (developing countries),

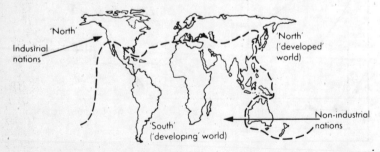

Fig. D.5 The North – South divide

with low incomes, malnutrition and illiteracy, and little hope of improvement since they have no more than 20 per cent of the world's wealth. The remaining 20 per cent of people live in a small group of wealthy, industrialised and highly armed countries (developed countries) in the so-called North (Fig. D.5). This smaller group of industrialised countries is increasingly dependent on the other group for its industrial supplies. Some of the indicators of the gap between developed and developing countries are:

- Birth rates – higher in 'developing' countries;
- Death rates – higher in 'developing' countries;
- The percentage of the population living in urban areas – lower in 'developing' countries;
- The size of the agricultural workforce – higher in 'developing' countries;
- The infant mortality rate – higher in 'developing' countries;
- Life expectancy – lower in 'developing' countries;
- The percentage of the child population enrolled in primary schools – lower in 'developing' countries;
- The energy consumption per person – lower in 'developing' countries;
- The calorie intake of food per person per day and daily meat consumption – lower in 'developing' countries;
- The number of newspapers sold per day per 1,000 people – lower in 'developing' countries;
- The average number of people per doctor – higher in 'developing' countries;
- The road density per area – lower in 'developing' countries;
- The percentage of adults who are literate – lower in 'developing' countries;
- The number of television sets per 1,000 people – this tends to be lower in 'developing' countries.

Fig. D.6 compares developing and developed countries.

	Brazil	China	India	UK
population (millions)	125	983	686	56
density (per sq km)	25	173	338	370
population growth (% per year)	2.8	1.9	2	0
infant mortality rate	92	56	122	12
life expectancy (yrs)	63	68	54	74
% living in urban areas	65	13	24	91
% literacy rate	76	N/A	36	98
TV sets (per 1,000 people)	98	9	1	390
energy production (million tonnes coal equivalent)	34	614	79	338

DISTANCE

energy consumption (million tonnes coal equivalent)	Brazil 94	China 565	India 126	UK 316
GNP $ per capita (or GDP)	1,881	290	232	8,900
% employed in agriculture	33	25	64	2
% employed in manufacturing industry	24	41	18	32
% employed in service industries	43	33	18	66
inflation rate (% per year)	101	7	13	12
area	35 times size of UK	39 times size of UK	13½ times size of UK	–

Fig. D.6 Comparing the development of three developing countries (Brazil, China and India) and one developed country (UK)

DISTANCE

Geographers use not only spatial distance (e.g., metres, kilometres) but also time distance (e.g., hours taken to complete a journey) and cost distance (e.g., the monetary cost of a journey). Fig. D.7 shows four different concepts of distance ('crow-fly' spatial distance; rail-track spatial distance; cost distance by train; time distance by train) as they apply to journeys to sixteen settlements from Norwich. Generally, spatial distance between places is constant over time. The building of new, more direct routes is the exception. Obviously, 'crow-fly' spatial distance is a constant. The building of the Humber Bridge reduced the spatial distance between East Yorkshire and North Lincolnshire settlements measured by the spatial distance of the road distance.

Time distances and cost distances have decreased enormously over time, particularly during this present century. Look at Fig. D.8, the time distance from Chicago map: it shows how the USA has shrunk in terms of time distance over the past 100 years. Improvements in speed of travel really have made the world a smaller place! From the standpoint of the length of journeys, the USA is about 200 times smaller than it was in 1880.

Electrification of British Rail lines at present will reduce the length of journeys and modify the time-distance map of Britain. It is interesting to note that for two journeys with the same spatial distance, their time distances can be significantly different. British Rail's Inter-City time-distance map shows that the 160 miles from London to Sheffield takes 150 minutes while the 188 miles from London to York takes 118 minutes.

Fig. D.9 shows transport costs plotted against distance for three forms of transport: road, rail and water. The cost of all forms of transport increases with spatial distance, but some forms are more expensive than others. Every day we see around us the results of the fact that road transport is the cheapest form of transport over short distances!

The effect that changes in cost distance have on the location and distribution of industries, shopping centres, towns, housing areas, etc. is considerable.

Distance influences the degree of interaction between places. As distance

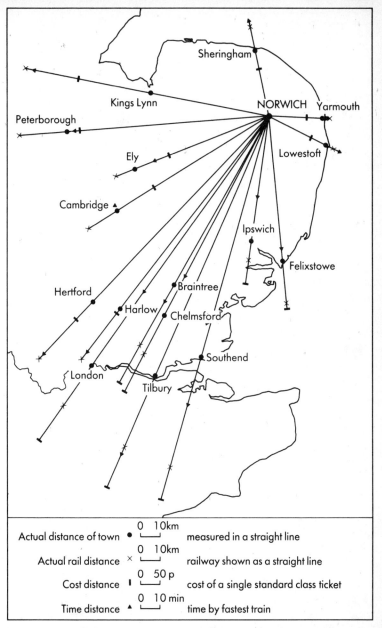

Actual distance of town ● ⊢—┘ 0 10km   measured in a straight line

Actual rail distance × ⊢—┘ 0 10km   railway shown as a straight line

Cost distance ▮ ⊢—┘ 0 50 p   cost of a single standard class ticket

Time distance ▲ ⊢—┘ 0 10 min   time by fastest train

Fig. D.7 Distances in East Anglia

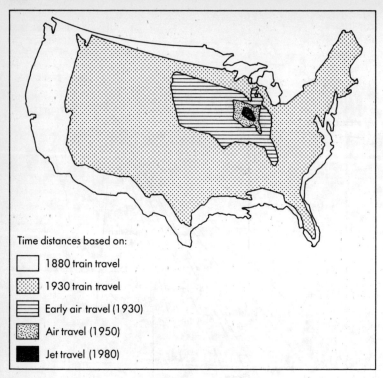

Time distances based on:

▢ 1880 train travel

▨ 1930 train travel

▤ Early air travel (1930)

▨ Air travel (1950)

■ Jet travel (1980)

Fig. D.8 Time distances from Chicago, 1880–1980

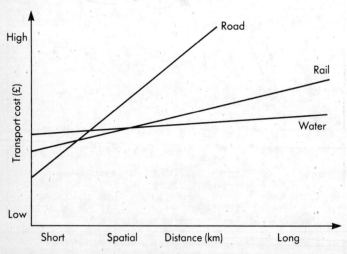

Fig. D.9 Comparison of transport costs/distance for road, rail and water transport (spatial, time or cost) between places increases, interaction between them tends to decrease. The idea that as distance increases, interaction and movement between places decreases is known as the friction of distance (or the distance-decay model). Spatial distance means separation, and that creates a barrier and inconvenience; time and costs are incurred in overcoming it. Tourist movement between places is an exception to the distance-decay model; more British holidaymakers visit Benidorm, Spain, than certain major British seaside resorts.

DISTRIBUTIONS

Geographers study the way in which the earth's surface changes. Population, resources, weather, soils, etc. have distributions across the space on the Earth's surface which can be shown on maps. Maps are spatial documents; they show spatial distributions. Geography is about spaces as well as places. Some of the patterns of distributions are general and recurring. For example, many urban areas conform to a general urban-land-use pattern (Fig. U.9), with certain forms of land use towards the centre and others towards the outside.

◄ Central Business District ►

DORMITORY TOWNS

◄ Commuting ►

DOWNLAND

◄ Escarpment ►

DRAINAGE BASINS

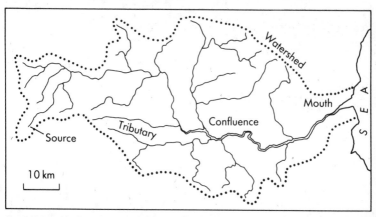

Fig. D.10 Drainage basin and watershed

A drainage basin is the catchment area for a river and so is composed of slopes, channels, etc. Drainage basins can be seen as integrated systems with inputs (e.g., rainfall) and outputs (e.g., streamflow into the sea). The boundary between separate basins is known as a watershed (Fig. D.10).

Watersheds change over time. They are both lowered and move backwards as the processes of erosion operate on the area (Fig. D.11).

Large drainage basins tend to have more gentle slopes, and steep basins tend to have a high stream frequency.

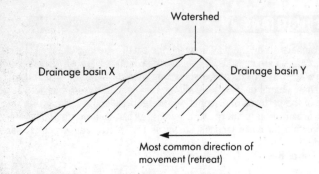

Fig. D.11 Changing watershed

DRAINAGE PATTERN

There are various patterns formed by the river and stream channels in an area (e.g., in a drainage basin). Three common patterns are dendritic, trellised (as in a type of garden fencing) and radial (like the spokes of a wheel) (Fig. D.12). Geology and relief (the shape of the ground) are generally responsible for the pattern formed by an area's drainage channels. For instance, a trellised drainage pattern often develops in an area where there are alternating outcrops of harder and softer rock. Valleys with drainage channels develop on the softer rock. On a dome-shaped upland such as the English Lake District or

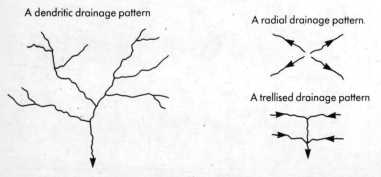

Fig. D.12 Three drainage patterns

a volcanic cone, streams and rivers will flow outwards and downhill from the centre and a radial drainage pattern will develop.

DRUMLINS

◀ Boulder clay ▶

EARTHQUAKES

An earthquake is a shaking movement or tremor among the rocks in the Earth's crust. Major earthquakes are the result of the geological plates which make up the Earth's crust slipping and sliding against each other. This suddenly releases stresses and pressures which have been accumulating over the time they have been locked together. The energy released by an earthquake is measured on the open-ended Richter Scale. The world's greatest quakes have reached 8 and above: for example, the 1906 San Francisco quake measured 8.3. The world's most earthquake-prone regions are around the rim of the Pacific, in Indonesia, south-west Asia and the eastern Mediterranean. Major earthquakes can occur where plate margins are grinding past each other, colliding together or pulling apart. More modest earthquakes can and do occur in Britain, along small, local faults with intensities of around 5 on the Richter Scale. When an earthquake occurs waves vibrate swiftly in all directions from the focus deep in the Earth's crust (Fig. E.1). These can be recorded by a seismograph. Fig. E.2 is a tracing of a distant earthquake.

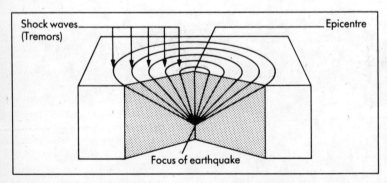

Fig. E.1 Cross-section of an earthquake

Major earthquakes are normally natural disasters, particularly when occurring in heavily populated areas. The Tangshan earthquake in China in 1976, which had a magnitude of 7.6, killed 250,000 people, although only 114

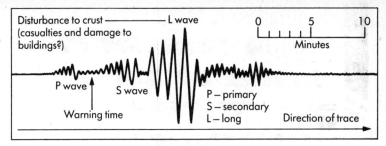

Fig. E.2 A seismograph recording of a distant earthquake

Why Mexico City was so vulnerable

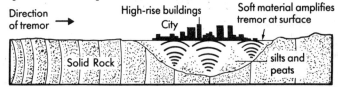

Fig. E.3 The 1985 Mexico City earthquake

died in the 8.6 quake in Alaska in 1964. Damage falls off as you move away from the epicentre, but much depends on the construction of buildings and the preparations that have been made in an area. Fig. E.3 shows why Mexico City was so vulnerable in 1985.

◀ Plate tectonics ▶

ECONOMIC DEVELOPMENT

Industry matters because industry and economic welfare/development go together. The more goods and services produced by industry and wanted by the community, the greater will be the community's wealth. Industry is wealth-producing activity which involves people in productive employment of all kinds: teaching, office work, factory jobs, etc. The best available indicator of the level of economic welfare in a country is provided by measuring the Gross National Product (GNP) per head. This per person value for the quantity of goods and services produced in a country in a year, assuming that the benefits are shared out equally among all citizens (we clearly know that they are not!), gives a guide to a country's wealth and its population's general standard of living. Fig. E.4 shows GNP per head of population for selected countries in 1986 and the way in which this information is used to divide countries into those with 'developing' economies and those with 'developed' economies.

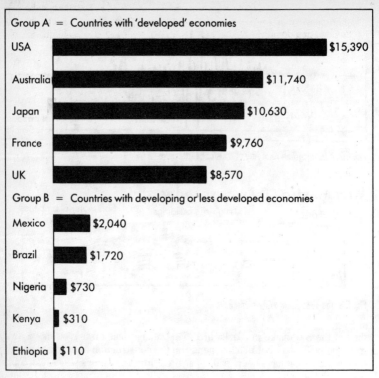

Fig. E.4 GNP per head of population for selected countries (1986)

Many of the high GNP per head or 'developed' countries are located in three centres of high industrialisation: Western Europe, North America and Japan. On the other hand, the so-called 'developing' countries, with their low or middle GNP per head figures are either newly industrialised, industrialising fast or have very little productive industry. It can be calculated from the information in the bar chart that people in many of the 'developing' countries receive in a year what an average citizen of the industrialised, 'developed' world might earn in a week. In the case of Ethiopia, its average annual income per person of $110 would only buy a dinner for two in some London restaurants. Wealth and industry clearly divide the world, a division which is shown by the 'North–South' map of the world (Fig. D.5).

There are two principal problems in using this measure of economic welfare to classify the countries of the world into groups:

- it does not measure human happiness and people's well-being. There is more to life than money and high human welfare is not necessarily associated with high economic welfare. People on low incomes in a 'developing' country may be as happy and satisfied with their lives as those on higher incomes in a 'developed' country;
- it is only an average and does not show up how wealth is distributed

among the population. Within every country there are both rich and poor people; in wealthy, industrialised countries like Britain there are pockets of poverty and some people with fairly low incomes. Equally, in a 'developing' country there may be a few people with very high incomes.

◀ Aid ▶

ECOSYSTEM

The term ecosystem refers to the interrelationships which exist between a set of living organisms in an area (plants and animals) and their non-living environmental surroundings (their habitat: e.g., climate, soil, slope, run-off, rock type, etc.). A pond can be seen as an ecosystem; each component of the pond environment, whether living or non-living, is linked together and interacts one with another to form a whole unit (a system). Ecosystems are open; each ecosystem is only a segment of the real world and is affected by and affects other parts of life.

ENERGY CRISIS

An energy crisis could face the world in the future in that it might become difficult to meet the ever-increasing demand for energy. Demand is expected to continue to increase yet supplies of our major sources of energy (the fossil fuels: coal and oil) have a limited life.

Energy sources can be classified as:

■ renewable – these are sources which cannot be exhausted, so their use does not reduce their supply: e.g., hydro-electricity, wind, solar power, tidal power;

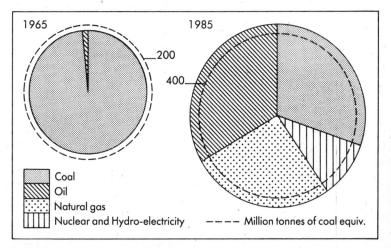

Fig. E.5 Primary energy consumption in Britain

- non-renewable – these are the exhaustible sources whose supply is fixed in quantity. Oil, natural gas and coal once burned, are lost to people.

Any future energy crisis will be a result of people's overdependence on non-renewable sources of energy.

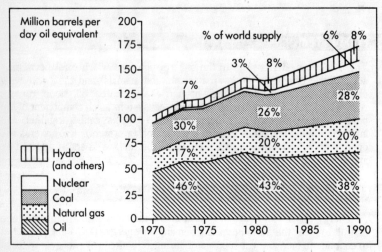

Fig. E.6 Changing world primary energy supplies, 1970–90

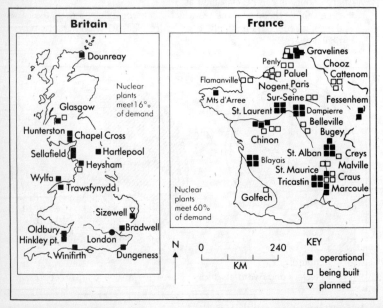

Fig. E.7 Nuclear power stations

There is a gradual switch in the world from fossil fuels: these made up 93 per cent of world supplies in 1973 and are predicted to fall to 86 per cent by 1990 (Figs. E.5 and E.6). Solar panels, wind farms, tidal barrages, wave power, geothermal (underground heat from the Earth's molten interior and volcanoes), dams for hydro-electric power projects and nuclear power stations (Fig. E.7) are areas for development. The last two of these raise objections from some people. The flooding of large areas of land behind dams built to generate hydro-electricity may leave many people homeless (e.g., the Sardar Sarova dam on the River Narmada in north-west India). In developed countries many people remain unconvinced about the safety of nuclear power production. However, unlike thermal power stations (coal- and oil-burning), they do not contribute to acid rain.

ENQUIRY

Enquiry is a way of thinking and working now very popular in geography. It involves students investigating, finding out and working out things for themselves, usually by following a sequence which starts with identifying a task very clearly and finishes with a conclusion/solution related closely to the original intention of the piece of work. Fieldwork in geography, where students gain first-hand experience of an environment and collect *original data* about it by observing and measuring (primary data), must be an enquiry. Enquiry work can also be undertaken on *secondary data* (data collected by someone else, such as that available in Census Returns or from the Meteorological Office).

ENTERPRISE ZONES

These were introduced by the British government in 1982 as part of their policy of offering financial incentives to industry to locate in areas of higher

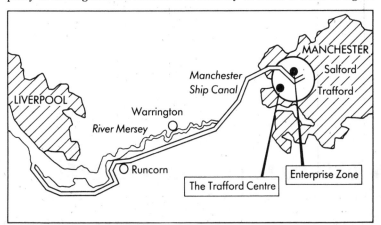

Fig. E.8 Manchester Docklands

unemployment. Parts of the following eleven places – Salford and Trafford, Liverpool, Wakefield (South Kirby), Hartlepool, Newcastle and Gateshead, Corby, Dudley, London (Isle of Dogs), Swansea, Belfast and Clydebank and Glasgow – were chosen to be additions to the **Assisted Areas** of the UK (Fig. A.9).

It is the run-down inner-city areas of these places that are the Enterprise Zones. This has led to some criticism from firms who had set up in the place but not in the new Enterprise Zone district.

Fig. E.8 shows the Trafford Park Enterprise Zone adjacent to Salford. Here the Trafford Park Development Corporation has been set up to help with the regeneration of 3,000 acres of former canalside (Manchester Docklands) and industrial land. In the process, it hopes to create thousands of jobs over the next few years.

EROSION

Areas of the Earth's surface are modified because rocks are broken down and worn away by the movement of water, ice, the sea, wind, people, machines, animals, etc. This destructive process is known as erosion (Fig. E.9). It includes the removal (transport) of the eroded debris to new locations. The surface agents which erode and sculpt the landscape do so in a number of different ways. Running water (rivers), for instance, moves rock particles of various sizes along the river bed in a process known as *hydraulic action*. This leads the particles to bang together as they move and so break up, and this is known as *attrition*. They bang against the bed and banks of the channel, so wearing it away, and this is known as *corrasion* or *abrasion*. Rivers also erode the bed and banks of their channels by *corrasion*, by the solution of soluble or partly soluble rocks.

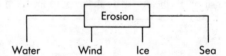

Fig. E.9

It has to be remembered that people and human economic activities are the most significant erosional force on the Earth's surface. Erosion is part of the continual cycle of decay–creation–decay–re-creation of landscapes, a cycle which includes **weathering** and **deposition**.

ESCARPMENT

The chalk Downs of southern England (e.g., Chiltern Hills, North Downs) include many two-slope upland features called escarpments.

Springs, places where water flows naturally out of the ground, are common on Downland. Around escarpments they can occur along the foot of both the scarp slope and the dip slope, at the junction of permeable chalk and the impermeable rock below, often clay. Chalk is permeable because it is porous, that is, composed of a mass of tiny air spaces that will fill with water rather than letting it drain away over the Earth's surface. The scenery of chalk Downlands is often described as 'scarp and vale', such areas normally have a dry but grassy, rolling appearance. 200-300 metres above sea level is normal for such areas. Settlements have often developed along the spring lines, as Fig. E.10 shows.

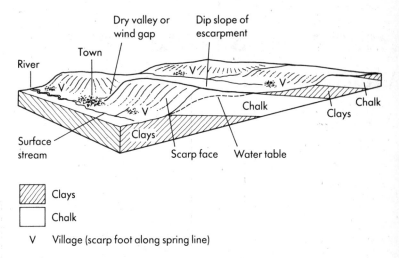

Fig E.10 Settlements developing along spring lines of escarpments

FAULTING

Faults are cracks or breaks in the rocks of the Earth's crust which form due to tectonic forces (forces originating inside the Earth and its crust). There must be subsequent movement of cracked/broken rock; one side of the fracture must slip downwards! This displacement of rock means that the two sides may not match. Faults vary in scale from small, single ones a few metres in size to large rift valleys and block mountains (horst) covering hundreds of miles. Fig. F.1 shows a block mountain surrounded by parallel step faults.

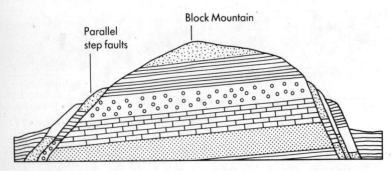

Fig. F.1 Faulting

FIORD

Coastlines along which fiords occur are described as *submergent*. Land has been flooded by a rise in sea level relative to land level; it has been submerged by water. A rise in sea level, perhaps because melting ice caps are adding water to the sea and/or because there has been a drop in land level has, say, along the Norwegian coast, drowned coastal troughs and valleys which had been cut by glaciers. A fiord is a drowned glaciated valley; it is a long, deep, narrow opening in the coast with steep, cliff-like sides. Fiords often are deeper inland than near their mouths; they, therefore, have fishing and harbouring possibilities as well as tourist potential.

FLOOD PLAIN

This is the flat land surrounding a river, usually in its lower course. The plain is formed of sediments once transported by the river and then deposited when it flooded its low banks. River channels on flood plains may be meandering, and **deposition** may have raised the height of the channel above the level of the surrounding flood plain. Such deposition as is found along the lower reaches of the River Mississippi is referred to as a levee (Fig. F.2).

◀ Meanders ▶

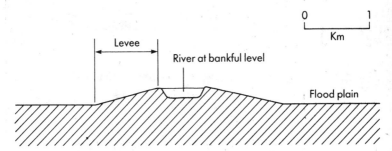

Fig. F.2 Flood plain

FOLD MOUNTAINS

Folding is a major tectonic (internal force from inside the Earth and its crust affecting the surface) process. It is the bending of a layer of rock. Rocks can be folded at a range of scales, from the small local scale (a bent layer of rock in a cliff face a few metres in size) through to the Continental scale; the Alps and the Himalayas are the result of rocks covering thousands of square miles being folded upwards. The Himalayas were thrown upwards by India and the Indian Plate drifting over the last 50 million years and colliding with Asia. Fold mountains result from compression where the boundaries of the plates that make up the Earth's crust collide and rocks and sediments are buckled

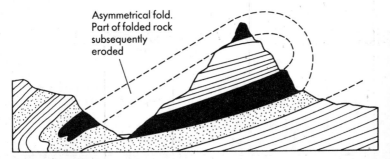

Fig. F.3 Fold mountains

upwards under the resulting enormous pressure. The world's fold mountains correspond with the location of the margins of the world's geological plates – those moving on a collision course. Any upfold is referred to as an *anticline*; a downfold is known as a *syncline*. Fold mountains are merely masses of giant anticlines, some symmetrical, where both limbs of the fold are of equal steepness, but mostly asymmetrical. **Erosion**, especially in high fold mountains as a result of glacial action, will subsequently modify the relief of the mountain as Fig. F.3 shows.

◀ Plate tectonics ▶

FOOD MOUNTAINS

◀ Common Agricultural Policy ▶

FOOD SUPPLY

Farming is the name given to people's use of their environment to produce food. Farms are the main source of food supply and also provide raw materials (e.g., wool) for manufacturing industry. Food is produced either for farmers and their families (*subsistence* farming) or for sale to other people (*commercial* farming).

In some **developing countries** growing crops and rearing livestock for food is a struggle and farming is mainly subsistence. Food shortages occur in the developing countries of Africa, Asia and South America.

World food production has grown faster than world population in recent years but about half of the food produced is eaten in the **developed countries**. These countries have only about a quarter of the world's population. Fig. F.4 shows the changes in food production, population and food production per head in both the developed and developing countries since 1955.

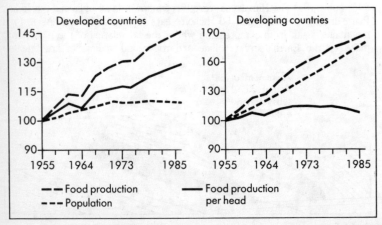

Fig F.4 Changes in food production and population

The changing demand for food matches changes in population and wealth. Farm production has to be increased to meet the ever increasing demand for food. There are two basic ways in which production can be increased:

- use more land for farming (agriculture);
- use farm land more productively so that yields (output from a certain area of land) rise.

The box below lists some recent United Nations recommendations for increasing world food supply. Giving everyone a healthy diet is at present partly a problem of distribution. There is a surplus of food in North America and Western Europe. In these developed countries farming can be called 'agri-business'; farmers work as businesspeople trying to increase their income by adapting their farming to the conditions and by trying to improve some of these conditions (e.g., the soil).

United Nations Recommendations for Increasing World Food Supply

1. Increase the present low level of human inputs into farming in developing countries (e.g., modern management methods, fertilisers, pesticides, technical equipment).
2. Grow crops more suited to local soils and climates in developing countries.
3. Grow crops in developing countries with higher calorie contents.
4. Use all the possible farmland for farming.
5. Encourage freer movement of food from areas of surplus to areas of shortage.

◄ Commercial farming, Subsistence farming ►

GENERAL CIRCULATION

The general circulation of the atmosphere is the broad pattern of general (not local) **winds**. It is a system of major winds whose basic object is the transfer of heat from the Equator, which receives more heat from the sun than it needs to maintain its present level of temperatures, towards the Poles, which would otherwise become progressively colder. The westerlies, the prevailing or predominant winds over Britain, are part of the general circulation.

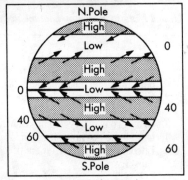

Fig. G.1 Belts of high and low pressure

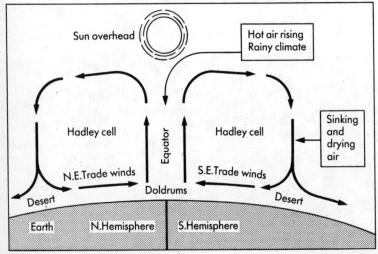

Fig. G.2 The tropical atmospheric circulation

The Earth's atmosphere can be divided, as Fig. G.1 shows, into alternate belts of permanent or semi-permanent high and low pressure. A belt of low pressure runs along the Equator; high pressure belts are centred round latitudes 60°N. and S., and there are high pressure regions, caused by sinking cold air at the Poles. Winds blow from the high to the low pressure areas but, due to the rotation of the Earth, swing to the right in the Northern Hemisphere and to the left in the Southern Hemisphere. This deflection as a result of the west–east rotation of the Earth is known as the *Coriolis Force* and is stated as Ferrel's Law. Thus a wind which would blow from north to south if the Earth were stationary becomes a north-easterly in the Northern Hemisphere.

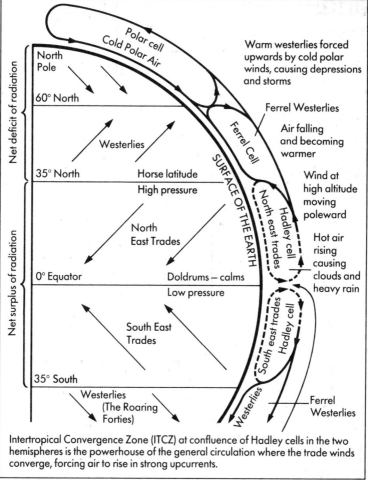

Intertropical Convergence Zone (ITCZ) at confluence of Hadley cells in the two hemispheres is the powerhouse of the general circulation where the trade winds converge, forcing air to rise in strong upcurrents.

Fig. G.3 The general circulation of the atmosphere

The most interesting part of the general circulation occurs between the two Tropics, where the circulations for each hemisphere meet. Figs. G.2 and G.3 show this part of the general circulation.

GLACIAL AREAS

◀ Boulder clay ▶

GLACIATED UPLAND

At present the Himalayas around Mount Everest are a glaciated upland. They lie above the snowline, the height above which the snow never melts. This height ranges from sea level at the Poles to around 5,500 metres (18,000 feet) at the Equator. Fig. G.4 shows three landform features – corrie, arête and pyramidal peak – which are typical of glaciated upland regions.

Between roughly 3 million and 20,000 years ago, Britain and north-west Europe experienced an Ice Age. At times, valley glaciers (rivers of ice) and ice sheets covered the whole of the British Isles north of the line from Bristol and London to a depth of 2,000 feet; only the tips of highland too low to have developed its own glaciers reached daylight! Ice flowed off the Scottish Highlands, the Welsh mountains and the Lake District. In these three upland areas existing landscape was considerably altered by the ice, especially by its erosional activity. Today they show landscape which is a legacy from the cold climate they experienced in the past. U-shaped valleys, corries (cwms or cirques), arêtes, pyramidal peaks, ribbon lakes, truncated spurs and moraines can be found.

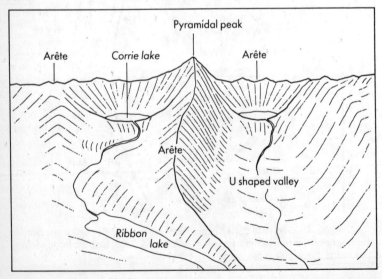

Fig. G.4 Typical glaciated upland

GRADIENT

A gradient is the slope of the land between any two points. It can be calculated from an Ordnance Survey map by finding the rise (or difference in height) between two points from the contours and measuring the horizontal distance between the points. Once the rise and horizontal distance are in the same unit (e.g., metres) they can be fitted into the following formula:

$$\text{Gradient} = \frac{\text{Rise}}{\text{Horizontal distance}}$$

The calculated gradient is stated either as a ratio (e.g., 1:100 or 1 in a 100) or as a percentage (e.g., 1 per cent). In both cases, for every 100 metres of horizontal distance there is a slope, either rise or fall, of 1 metre.

GREEN BELT

This is an area reserved for farming or recreation around an urban area or between towns/cities. Permission is not available for housing or factory building or any other form of urban development. The Green Belt is designed to act as a barrier to further **urbanisation** of the countryside, which steady **urban sprawl** would achieve.

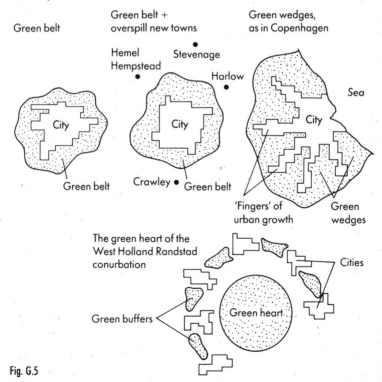

Fig. G.5

Some people object to the position of some Green Belts, especially if house building is being prevented when there is a general shortage of housing in the area (e.g., the North Downs Green Belt and the nearby London housing shortage).

Fig. G.5 shows the Green Belt and variations on it – green wedge, green buffer and green heart.

GREEN REVOLUTION

The term has been used since the 1960s to describe the attempts to improve farming and the food problems of **developing countries**. New fast-growing and high-yielding varieties such as IR8 rice have been developed.

India, especially the state of Punjab, is a good example of the success of the 'green revolution'. Over the past twenty years crop yields per hectare and grain production have grown faster than population, and the use of fertilisers and irrigation has grown significantly. There have been problems though:

- educating farmers in new methods;
- high-yielding varieties require the correct dose of expensive chemical fertiliser and weedkiller;
- the maintenance and high running-costs of technical equipment (e.g., irrigation pumps, cultivators).

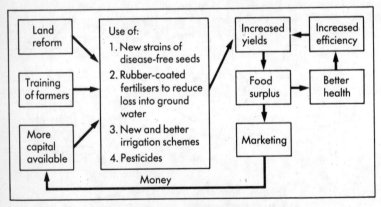

Fig G.6 Green revolution developments in developing countries

Many areas have the possibility of much greater output, particularly when there is investment in fertilisers, pesticides, technical equipment and modern management methods (Fig. G.6). Crops such as coffee and strawberries are grown productively in places, with the aid of these inputs, for export to developed countries. More financial aid for farming and food markets which give better prices to farmers may help to increase the supply of food for the local population.

GREENFIELD SITE

Two types of land for industrial development are recognised at the present time: greenfield and brownfield. Greenfield tends to be the more popular. One of the reasons that the Toyota car company chose Burnaston, south Derbyshire, rather than Sheffield for its UK car assembly plant was that the former was a greenfield site while the Sheffield site was brownfield. A greenfield site is on land that has previously not been used for industrial or urban development; it is likely to be in the countryside or on the edge of an urban area. A brownfield site, on the other hand, will be an old industrial site on land formerly occupied by industry or housing. The derelict land in Sheffield's former steel industry area, the Lower Don Valley, constitutes a brownfield site.

Today's 'sunrise industries', using and producing high-tech equipment such as computers, lasers, micro-electronics, favour greenfield sites. A high-quality environment with green open space around has become a locational factor for manufacturing industry. Modern manufacturing tends to be light (makes small, easily transported items) and footloose but transport-dependent; the locations chosen are often on greenland in pleasant environments close to motorway junctions.

◀ Science (technology) parks ▶

GREENHOUSE EFFECT

A term to describe the increase in the atmosphere of gases, largely as a result of industrial pollution, which possess the 'greenhouse' property. Heat from the sun is radiated on to the Earth's surface, where it changes its wavelength from short, ultra-violet to long, infra-red radiation and bounces back into space. 'Greenhouse gases' let the sun's rays through but slow down the escape of radiation from the Earth to space. More of the Earth's own heat is trapped. The 'greenhouse gases' are carbon dioxide, methane, nitrous oxide, ozone and chlorofluorocarbons, and the by-products of industry, agriculture and the burning of fossil fuels such as coal and oil. Carbon dioxide is the largest single greenhouse gas, and is thought to have increased its presence in the atmosphere by 25 per cent over the past 200 years and to be continuing that increase (Fig. G.7).

The 'greenhouse effect' is generally believed to exist but as yet there is no conclusive evidence that people's activities are warming up the planet. Global temperature is higher now than it has been since records began and is believed to have increased by 0.5°C since 1900 (Fig. G.8). Greenhouse gases *may* increase average global temperature by 1.5 to 5°C by 2050. Warming caused by people changing the Earth's atmosphere threatens to have drastic effects. For example, raising sea levels would drown millions of square kilometres of fertile land; a 3 to 5°C increase in temperature may cause a 50 to 165 cm sea level rise, largely through the melting of the Polar ice caps. Millions of people live on the world's great river deltas – the Nile, Ganges, Mekong, Yangzte and Mississippi – and would lose their land and homes. The map of Britain would also be different.

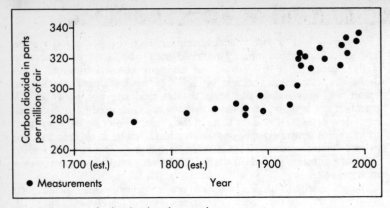

Fig. G.7 The amount of carbon dioxide in the atmosphere

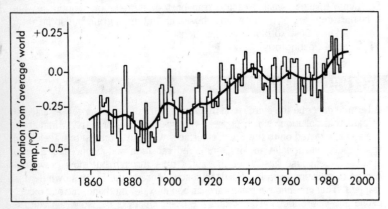

Fig. G.8 Global surface air temperature

However, predicting how the 'greenhouse effect' is likely to affect the climate of any place is still very uncertain (Fig. G.9). More heat in the Earth's weather system may lead to any one country becoming wetter or drier, warmer or colder. Our understanding is sketchy but it is thought that the effects on the weather will be uneven and subtle. Britain might experience more dry, hot summers and mild winters; an increasingly Mediterranean climate in which a 'café culture' could develop but fresh water in summer would be scarce. On the other hand, Britain might cool down as the ocean currents move.

What would really matter is any rainfall and temperature change in the main food-producing areas such as the American Prairies, the Indian monsoon belt, etc. Action to curb the emission of carbon dioxide and the destruction of forests may ease the problem. Burning trees produces more carbon dioxide.

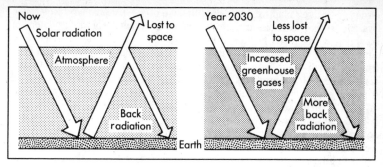

Fig. G.9 Possible results of the 'greenhouse effect'

Trees also remove carbon dioxide from the atmosphere through photosynthesis. The oceans also absorb carbon dioxide, but how much is not known, and if the world's climates do become warmer, will more cloud be produced, so cutting out more solar radiation and thus leading to cooling?
◀ Deforestation, Ozone layer ▶

GRID REFERENCES

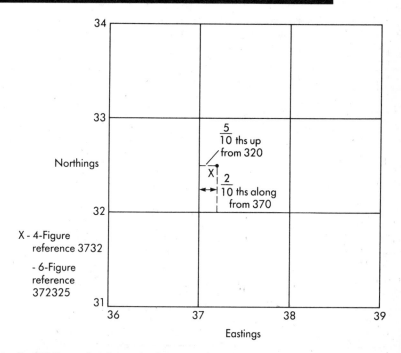

Fig. G.10 How to obtain four- and six-figure map references

Ordnance Survey map work requires the use of the National Grid Reference System so that locations can be pinpointed precisely. This is a system of numbered vertical and horizontal lines. Britain is divided into 100 kilometre squares, each then subdivided into one-kilometre squares. The vertical lines (running north–south) are known as eastings, because they indicate the distance east of the system's origin in the Scilly Isles. The horizontal lines (running east–west) are referred to as northings, because they indicate distance north of the origin. To refer to a specific kilometre square, work from bottom left and give the easting followed by the northing. For greater accuracy than a four-figure reference, a third figure may be added to the right-hand of each part of the reference. This third figure is obtained by estimating how many tenths the point in question is east of the easting and north of the northing. A six-figure reference is then produced (Fig. G.10).

GROSS NATIONAL PRODUCT

◀ Economic development ▶

GROWTH POLE

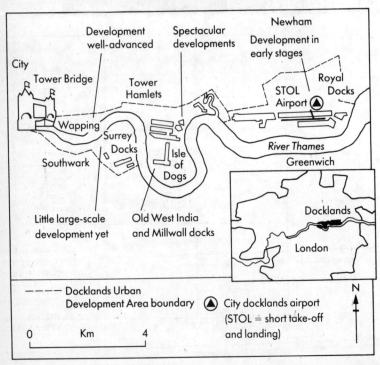

Fig. G.11 The London Docklands area

This term is used to describe the economic core of an area (region, country, continent). The core will be a centre of investment and industrial development; the area will be one of growing and new industry and general prosperity. Wealth and ideas will spread outwards from this core towards the economically peripheral areas. A so-called 'golden triangle' running from southern Germany (Munich) towards northern Italy (Milan) and Switzerland and then on towards Paris/Brussels and back to Munich is generally regarded as the growth pole of Europe.

Within Britain the 8-square-mile London Docklands area (Fig. G.11) is becoming a growth pole, growing by a process known as cumulative causation (Fig. G.12). For the twenty or so years before this development, the area was in a vicious circle of decline: cumulative causation in reverse. Since the 1960s the London Docks and dock-related industries have been closing down, leaving a large area of land near the city centre suitable for redevelopment. The government formed the London Docklands Development Corporation to be responsible for the redevelopment by spending government money given to the project and by attracting private property developers. One spectacular plan is the building of eighty-storey office towers at Canary Wharf on the Isle of Dogs with a view to persuading some of the financial institutions of the City to move to them. There would be office space for thousands of new or transferred jobs. Certain people have argued that this development, while benefiting some, has not been of value to the local people.

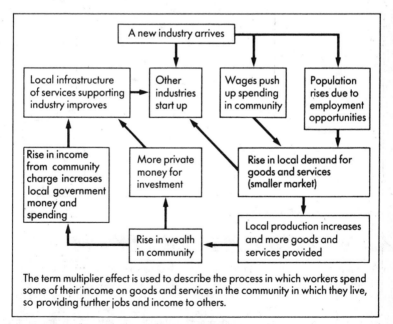

Fig. G.12 The growth or decline of a region by cumulative causation

HEAT ISLAND

This is a meteorologist's term for large urban areas which tend to have temperatures several degrees warmer than surrounding rural areas. The heat island effect is perhaps most significant at night and during winter months, and is demonstrated by the way that snow, for example, settles for shorter periods in cities. Industrial plants, heated office buildings, houses and vehicles all contribute heat to the city air. There is less heat loss in cities as a result of moisture evaporation from the ground; there is less evaporation taking place because of drainage systems, which means less heat loss than there would be if there were no artificial drainage. Wind speeds are lower in urban areas; reduced wind speed means reduced heat loss. Urban buildings absorb heat during the daytime; this absorbed heat is eventually radiated.

Fig H.1 shows the heat island effects in Sheffield.

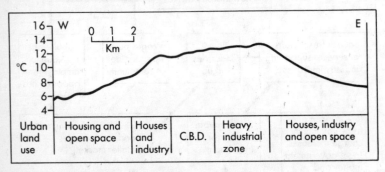

Fig. H.1 Sheffield's heat island effect, May 1986

HIERARCHY

A hierarchy is an order of importance which could be based, for instance, on size. Settlements can be ranked in order of their importance with the largest or most important first. A settlement hierarchy based on size would be conurbations, city, industrial town, market town, village, hamlet and farmstead; that is, arranged in order of population size from largest to smallest.

Population size is usually related to the number of services/functions that the settlement provides. Fig. H.2 shows that:

- the further up the hierarchy a settlement is, the more services it provides and the higher the order of those services that are available. Only cities provide infrequently used, high-order services such as wedding dress shops!
- the further up the hierarchy a settlement is, the fewer there are of them. There are many villages and few cities. The settlement hierarchy can be drawn as a pyramid, with hamlets and villages forming the wide base and cities and conurbations the narrow peak.

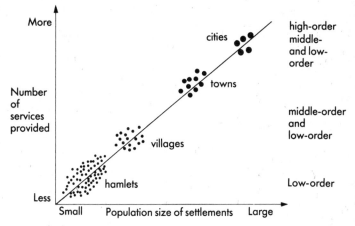

Fig. H.2 Settlement hierarchy

It is possible to rank the settlements in an area or a country according to their population size and then see if the hierarchy conforms to the rank–size rule. This geographical theory says that the second settlement in the hierarchy will be half the size of the largest, the third settlement one-third the size of the largest, and so on downwards. The rule does not fit many areas or countries. For example, in the USA a number of large settlements dominate the top of the hierarchy (e.g., New York, Los Angeles, Chicago). In many developing countries there is a primate city which is three or four times larger than the next city down the hierarchy (e.g., Mexico City, Mexico; Montevideo, Uruguay, etc.).

HIGH-TECH INDUSTRY

The term 'sunbelt' has been used to describe areas in which industry is booming (sun-rise industries) and there is growing prosperity. This can occur at a number of scales: regions within countries, countries and groups of countries. In Britain the so-called M4 'silicon corridor' to the west of London and in the USA California's Silicon Valley south of San Francisco towards San José and the area around Atlanta, Georgia have been described as 'sunbelts'.

There is also a developing area of advanced industrial activity, a 'sunbelt' in East Anglia. Modern high-tech industries (electronics) and large service industries are being attracted to areas surrounding the London–Cambridge motorway (M11). The development of nearly 400 new small science- and technology-based firms in Cambridge, including the opening of the Cambridge Science Park, during the past decade has been called the 'Cambridge phenomenon' and is transforming an area which once had little manufacturing. Links with the city's university and its scientific brains and links between firms are very strong. The area's other attractions are;

- the combined effect of the M11 and M25 (London Orbital) motorways;
- the expansion of Stansted airport into a major international airport;
- the availability of land for industrial purposes at prices lower than elsewhere in south-east England (industrial land in East Anglia is about a quarter of the price of that along the so-called M4 corridor in Berkshire and very little more than in the north of England).

Transport improvements are helping to cause a change in the economic and social lifestyle of many **developed countries**. Motorways and important dual carriageways are leading to the development of light manufacturing industry, as in the M27 corridor (Fig. H.3). Modern manufacturing industries like electronic and computer companies in Britain are tending not to start up in the old urban industrial centres like Liverpool, Sheffield and Glasgow, but in market towns like Winchester and Bury St Edmunds, where unemployment is lower and population growing. Bury St Edmunds has a 6.7 per cent unemployment rate and a 17 per cent population growth rate. The average

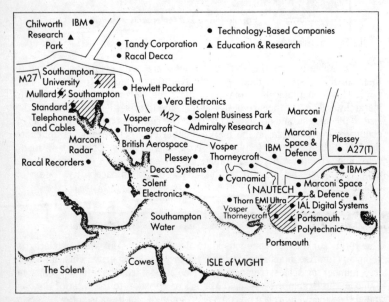

Fig. H.3 The M27 corridor

unemployment rate for Britain's large cities is 16 per cent; their populations are generally declining. Improving quality of life is the other reason, in addition to the 'motorway effect', often given by industrialists for setting up in smaller market towns.

◀ Intermediate technology, Science (technology) parks ▶

HONEYPOT AREA

The term is used in geography to describe tourist areas luxurious in comparison to the region/country that surrounds them. With the development of a tourist industry in low-income, developing countries such as the West Indian islands and Kenya, with their tropical climates, has come the development of honeypot resorts, vastly different from the rest of the country.

Tourism is now Jamaica's second biggest earner of foreign currency. The present importance of tourism is clearly linked with the weather and climate experienced by the island. Most visitors to the West Indian islands are part of the 'sun rush' from affluent USA, Canada and Western Europe (Fig. H.4). Some people in the **developed countries** are willing and able to pay large sums of money to travel long distances to spend their greater leisure time in an environment very different both physically (weather, scenery, etc.) and culturally (lifestyle of the people, etc.) from that of their home country. Holidays have become to some people more of a necessity than a luxury.

Sources of foreign earnings (Jamaica)	1965	1985
bauxite and aluminium exports	39%	48%
sugar and sugar product exports	29%	10%
tourism	17%	26%
banana exports	6%	4%
others	9%	12%

Climatic factor	Jan.	July	Annual average
ave. day temp. (°C)	24.4	27.2	26.1
rainfall (mm)	22.9	38.1	800.1
daily sunshine (hours)	7.9	7.9	7.4

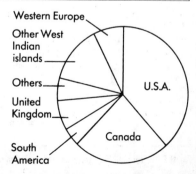

Fig. H.4 The origin of tourist visitors to the West Indies, 1985

Kenya, with its game parks and beach resorts along the Indian Ocean shore, is an example of the attraction that a different physical and cultural environment has for people living in Western Europe. The number of foreign tourists has increased a hundred times in the past thirty years, and tourism is now Kenya's third biggest earner of foreign currency, making a large contribution to the country's economy. Cheaper flights have made Kenya more accessible to many West Europeans. It is planned to use the money provided by this tertiary industry to develop a broader industrial base. However, the development of a tourist industry can bring both benefits and problems to the local people. Tourists spending has a multiplier effect on the local area. More jobs and a higher level of economic welfare may be created generally, but the benefits may not be fully available to all the people.

HOSTILE ENVIRONMENT

This is the name given to a region of the world in which natural conditions, particularly climate, are unwelcoming for people; they are inhospitable places. There are five regions hostile to close human settlement and so sparsely populated. These are:
- the polar ice deserts of Antarctica and the North Pole region;
- the tundra (edge of the ice caps) and taiga (coniferous pine forest) regions of Scandinavia, North Canada and the Soviet Union;
- the hot deserts of Africa, Australia and the Middle East;
- the hot, wet equatorial forests of Brazil, the East Indies and Central Africa;

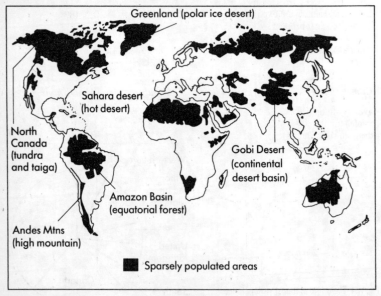

Fig. H.5 The correlation between sparse population and hostile environment

- desert basins (e.g., south-west USA) and high mountains, especially those in the deep interiors of continents.

These sparsely populated areas are shown in Fig. H.5 where one example of each type of hostile environment is indicated. Expensive high technology can make an environment a little less hostile for living, but generally this occurs only where valuable natural resources can be extracted. For example, developed world oil companies provide a slightly more comfortable environment for their workers in the Middle Eastern deserts. The large oil revenues received by Middle East countries such as Saudi Arabia and Kuwait have enabled them to pay for technology to modify the desert environment in places (e.g., air-conditioned city buildings, imported water supplies and even 'greening' of the desert). Expensive, highly irrigated wheat grows in parts of the Arabian desert.

◀ Population density ▶

HURRICANE

A hurricane is a violent, revolving tropical storm, with winds reaching force 12 on the Beaufort Scale (up to 100 mph). Dense, dark thunderstorm clouds and very heavy rain mark the passage of a hurricane. They are experienced in the Gulf of Mexico region (West Indies, Central America, Texas) in late summer and leave behind them a trail of destruction, especially when at full strength and when crossing areas not well adapted to minimising their effects (e.g., certain of the least developed West Indian islands). Hurricanes are tropical cyclones, not dissimilar to temperate depressions.

HYDROGRAPH

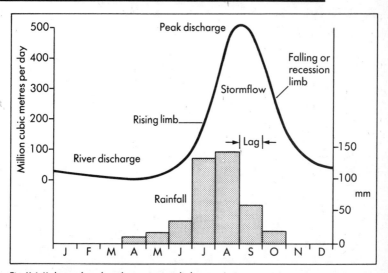

Fig. H.6 Hydrograph to show changes in river discharge over time

Fig. H.6 is a diagram drawn to show the changes in the discharge of a river over a period of time. The discharge (or streamflow) data can be graphed either as bars or a line. The shape of a hydrograph will be affected by **rainfall** in the river's drainage basin, so many hydrograph diagrams include rainfall data also plotted against *time*. Fig. H.7 shows a time lag or delay between the wettest period of the year and the hydrograph peak. This is normal.

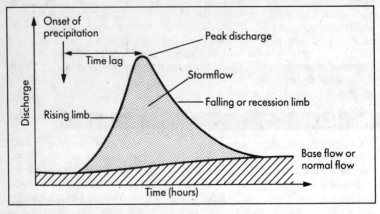

Fig. H.7 A storm hydrograph

ICE AGE

◀ Glaciated upland ▶

INDUSTRIAL ESTATES

Leicester City Council, like many other local authorities in Britain, recognises four types of industrial area within the city: backyard, neighbourhood, concentrated and estate (Fig. I.1). It is the policy of the City Council to concentrate new industrial development for the most part on the fourth type, industrial estates. The segregation of industrial and residential areas can be achieved if local governments build industrial estates. These may mean that manufacturers do not have a choice of location within the city/town, because permission to develop on sites other than the industrial estate may be refused.

Type	Main features
1 backyard	■ isolated pockets throughout older residential areas ■ small-scale firms of house size ■ cheap rents
2 neighbourhood	■ medium-large plants surrounded by housing ■ typical of inner-city areas drawing labour from immediate locality
3 concentrated	■ old firms (19th and early 20th century) ■ separated from residential areas ■ directly accessible to major traffic routes
4 estate	■ large, modern and landscaped ■ planned with services provided (water supply, electricity, gas, telecommunications, off-street car parking, etc.) ■ locationally well sited

Fig. I.1 Types of industrial area in Leicester

Fig. I.2 shows the location, within the city, of Sheffield's thirty major industrial estates. The importance of road transport, the clustering of estates in the old industrial areas of the Lower Don Valley, and the edge-of-city

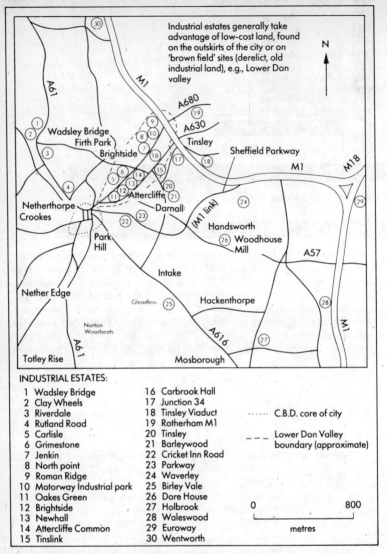

Industrial estates generally take advantage of low-cost land, found on the outskirts of the city or on 'brown field' sites (derelict, old industrial land), e.g., Lower Don valley

INDUSTRIAL ESTATES:

1 Wadsley Bridge
2 Clay Wheels
3 Riverdale
4 Rutland Road
5 Carlisle
6 Grimestone
7 Jenkin
8 North point
9 Roman Ridge
10 Motorway Industrial park
11 Oakes Green
12 Brightside
13 Newhall
14 Attercliffe Common
15 Tinslink
16 Carbrook Hall
17 Junction 34
18 Tinsley Viaduct
19 Rotherham M1
20 Tinsley
21 Barleywood
22 Cricket Inn Road
23 Parkway
24 Waverley
25 Birley Vale
26 Dore House
27 Holbrook
28 Waleswood
29 Euroway
30 Wentworth

······ C.B.D. core of city

‒ ‒ ‒ Lower Don Valley boundary (approximate)

0   800

metres

Fig. I.2 Sheffield's major industrial estates

location of many estates can be seen. A study of the Roman Ridge Industrial Estate (Fig. I.3) shows its good road transport facilities, especially its accessibility to the M1 motorway. The estate was designed almost entirely for light industry and service industry. There are small factory units producing glass, laboratory equipment, industrial diamonds and frozen food, small warehouses and cold stores.

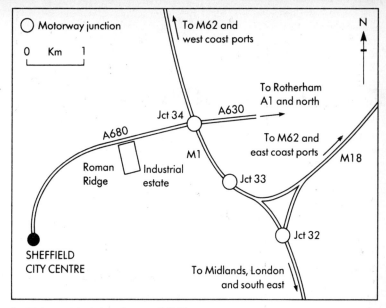

Fig. I.3 Roman Ridge Industrial Estate, Sheffield

A study of the industries locating on most industrial estates shows that they are often:

- 'footloose' light industries, with no particular orientation to materials or to specific markets, transport improvements having reduced the importance of the old factors of nearness to materials or markets;
- directly consumer-based industries dependent on road transport, especially for the distribution of products;
- small- or medium-sized firms employing relatively few people.

Types of industry	Number of factory units occupied	Total number of employers	Example
general engineering and metal	25	453	precision tools
plastics	6	43	window systems
food processing	10	131	frozen foods, soft drinks
timber and paper	4	19	woodwares
warehousing, packaging and distribution	6	76	Pickfords (national freight consortium)
others, inc. service industries and unoccupied	13	164	florist, contractor, petrol pump servicing
total	64	886	

Fig. I.4 A survey of firms on the Chesterfield Trading Estate

A survey of Chesterfield Trading Estate, a former greenfield site now located next to the Sheffield–Chesterfield dual carriageway, shows that it consists of sixty-four factory units as shown in Fig. I.4.

◀ Greenfield sites ▶

INDUSTRIAL INERTIA

This term describes the situation when industries remain where they were originally sited, even though the initial reasons for location at that point (e.g., water, power, proximity to a canal or a coalfield) are no longer of any importance. Maybe the industry would be better positioned beside a motorway, for example, but the expense involved in relocation is too great. Steelworks on old, inland sites close to coalfields might be an example of inertia. Sheffield's remaining steelworks may be locationally inert, but in some cases factors such as local expertise and closeness to the motorway may mean Sheffield remains a suitable location.

INDUSTRIAL LOCATIONS

The location of industrial activities may be influenced by a whole range of factors: raw materials, labour supply, government policy, markets, etc. (Fig. I.5). There have been various attempts made by geographers to develop a general explanation for the locations chosen. Three types of location have been recognised, as shown in the table below: material-orientated, market-orientated and footloose (or randomly located).

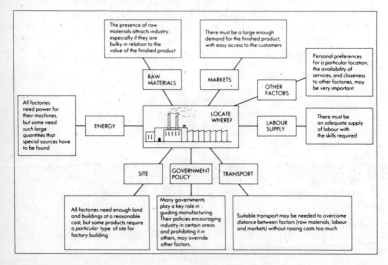

Fig. I.5 Some factors influencing the location of manufacturing

Group	Characteristic
material-orientated	located near the source of the raw materials they process
market-orientated	located near their consumers
footloose	free from the restriction of materials and markets and not tied to any location

Brickworks, pulp and paper mills, and sugar beet factories tend to be material-orientated; production is carried out near to the source of the raw material (primary product) they process. These are weight-losing industries; it is more costly to transport the raw material than the finished product, so by locating close to the source of the materials, transport costs are saved. Market-orientated industries are those close to their customers and also a large workforce. Bakeries, breweries, motor car assembly plants, etc. are located in urban areas because it is generally cheaper for them to produce there. Many modern industries are footloose and tied neither to where their materials nor their markets are.

The results of a recent survey of 2,000 newly founded companies in the USA (see the table) show how important factors other than hard financial considerations are in the industrial location decision.

Earning sufficient rather than going for the largest possible profits may determine how industrialists actually think. There may be a wide geographical area in which they can do this, because of the improvement of transport facilities, and so the choosing of a place within an area may be guided by a variety of additional factors: government regional policy, the image and environment of the place, the layout of the motorway network, initiatives taken by local authorities such as advertising, hospitalities, etc.

Rank	Reasons for location choice
1	personal reasons (e.g., home town of manufacturer)
2	close to markets
3	access to other plants (i.e., trade links and production relationships)
4	suitable buildings and/or site at favourable price
5	close to raw materials
6	suitable labour at favourable wage rates
7	assistance or encouragement by local groups
8	suitable transport facilities

INFANT MORTALITY

◀ Life expectancy ▶

INFRASTRUCTURE

This term is used to cover all the vital public services that have to be available in an area before industrial production can take place. A basic network of communications, power and water supplies, schools, hospitals and other facilities are needed before any large-scale production and economic development can occur. A **transport network** with a reasonably high degree of **connectivity** is an absolute requirement for economic development.

Development in **developing countries** is often hindered by lack of such infrastructure. Much investment has gone into developing an infrastructure of roads, water supplies, etc. in some of the oil-rich countries such as Saudi Arabia.

In Britain, infrastructure is basically part of the public sector; its full provision on **industrial estates** is usually regarded as a responsibility of the local authority.

INNER CITY

Between the **central business district** and the outer residential suburbs of a city lies a large area loosely called the inner city. It can include a variety of land

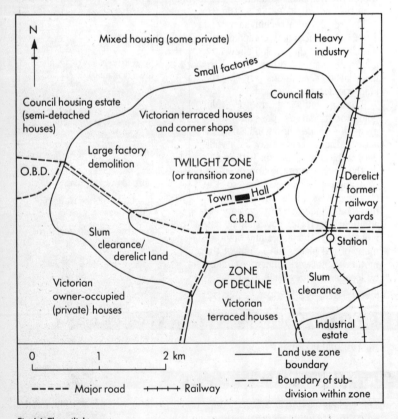

Fig. I.6 The twilight zone

uses but it is normally associated with a run-down environment showing signs of urban decay and is in need of urban renewal/redevelopment. The term *twilight zone* has been used to describe those parts of the inner city with their below-standard residential environment.

Twilight zones such as the one shown in Fig. I.6 are generally areas of old manufacturing industry, warehousing and cheap, terraced housing built close to the old factories in the last century. Some may now be unfit to live in. Over the past twenty or thirty years many local authorities in the large industrial cities have tried to improve the environment of their inner-city areas. In places, buildings were demolished and there is now derelict and rubble-strewn land because the land has not been reused. So-called brownfield sites are not as popular with industry as **greenfield sites**. Some local authorities have plans for new industry, parkland and new housing on this land. In other inner-city areas local planners have tried to make the area a better and safer place without removing any of the existing buildings. This is known as urban renewal, as opposed to urban redevelopment, which involves pulling down buildings and building a completely replanned area.

Inner-city areas, though they traditionally have the highest **population density** – small, tightly packed houses – have been losing population in recent years. This can be seen in Fig. I.7.

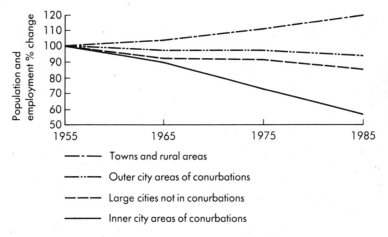

Fig. I.7 The change in population and employment in four types of area in Britain between 1955 and 1985

This declining population reflects the loss of employment in many inner-city manufacturing industries. However, in some cities urban ghettos develop. People, some born outside the country, live together as an almost closed community with poor opportunities and amenities and many find themselves trapped in the area. Urban ghettos are found in Inner London and large cities in the USA, and are characterised by substandard housing, overcrowding, neglected amenities, high levels of delinquency, crime and violence and common cultural experiences, perhaps a shared ethnic background.

The British government has recently developed plans to improve conditions in some of the most run-down inner-city areas, and to tackle their problems of high unemployment, crime, and unused and underused land. Urban Development Corporations exist in the London Docklands, Merseyside, Trafford Park, Teeside, Tyne and Wearside, Sheffield and the Black Country. Assisted Area policy, including **Enterprise Zones**, also focus attention on the renewal of inner-city areas.

◀ Assisted areas ▶

INTENSITY OF CULTIVATION

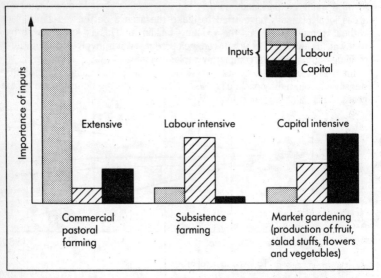

Fig. I.8 Inputs of land, labour and capital needed for three types of farming

Each type of farming has a different system and inputs and processes will vary, as will the outputs. The different types of farming often require different inputs. Fig. I.8 shows combinations of inputs of land, labour and capital (money invested in buildings and equipment) needed for three types of farming. When a high proportion of land is used in relation to labour and capital, the farm is described as extensive. Intensive farms use a high proportion of either labour or capital in relation to land. Extensive farms are large and sometimes use marginal farming land (land which is only just agriculturally productive). Intensive farms are smaller and often found in densely populated areas. The land is intensively used and produces high yields because of high mechanisation or the employment of a relatively large labour force. Fig. I.9 shows how various farming types relate to the two systems.

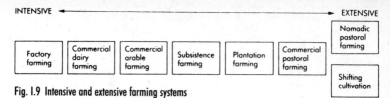

Fig. I.9 Intensive and extensive farming systems

INTERLOCKING SPURS

These are river valley features normally found in the upper courses of rivers in upland areas. The river channel follows a winding course around the foot of spurs which seem to 'lock' into each other from both sides (Fig. I.10).

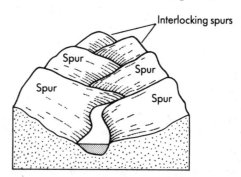

Fig. I.10

INTERMEDIATE TECHNOLOGY

Technology refers to people's use of tools and machinery. High-tech industry uses highly sophisticated, complex technology such as computers, micro-electronics, robots and lasers. This is the way of the future in developed countries. On the other hand, in developing countries keen to industrialise, more appropriate technology than high-tech may be intermediate technology, that is, simple, easily maintained and cheaply produced machines. Highly technologically advanced tractors that villagers in Africa cannot repair, perhaps through lack of spare parts, is *not* appropriate technology.

Africa is not naturally poor in an economic sense; it has many industrially significant raw materials (e.g., chrome, manganese, uranium, oil, natural gas, platinum, etc.), but it has become a primary producer (a producer of commodities/raw materials) rather than a manufacturing producer (a producer of goods). Rather than process the materials themselves into manufactured goods they tend to export them to the 'developed' industrial countries for processing. Fig. I.11 shows this pattern of world trade between the developed and developing countries for India. To take a developed country as an example, Japan depends on imports of iron from India, wood and rubber from Malaysia, copper from the Philippines and Papua New Guinea, petroleum from Indonesia and cotton from Mexico. Some developing countries were

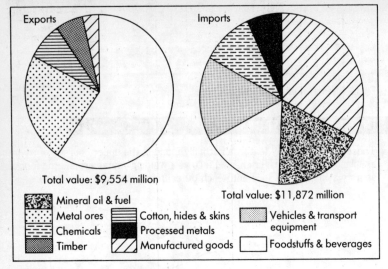

Fig. I.11 Export and import trade of India, 1985

organised during their colonial past (Britain, France, Germany, Italy and Spain colonised Africa during the nineteenth century) to supply raw materials for the manufacturing industries of the colonial masters and provide a market for their manufactured products.

A further problem today for the primary producers of the developing world is that world trade is arranged so that their primary products sell at cheap prices in the developed countries.

Many developing countries are keen to develop manufacturing industries; most depend heavily on agriculture and have less than a quarter of their workers in manufacturing. Kenya, for instance, is an overwhelmingly agricultural economy in which manufacturing contributes 13 per cent to the GNP, a relatively high figure in Africa. Small-scale and cottage industries, often located in villages, make up a significant proportion of this manufacturing output.

Wood-carving co-operatives (where groups of people pool everything) are an example of the sort of small-scale manufacturing employing large numbers of people which is actively encouraged by the governments of many developing countries. The cottage industry or domestic system existed in early eighteenth-century Britain and still exists in many developing countries today. It involves people, often craftsmen and craftswomen, working in their own homes or small workshops with raw materials supplied by a merchant or middleman, who will also collect the finished goods and make arrangements for their sale. Unlike a factory, the processing occurs in different places. Cloth and clothing; basket, rug and mat making, footwear, pottery and metal goods are typical cottage industries, especially in South-East Asia.

Most developing countries have been trying to develop manufacturing industry in order to increase the level of economic welfare of their people, but they have faced problems in doing so. Many of these countries have produced, since their independence from colonialism, a series of national development plans. The Fourth National Development Plan for Nigeria, 1981–5, recognises the importance of using the money from their oil exports to develop economically by:

- encouraging the rapid growth of manufacturing;
- providing facilities and services for industry (infrastructure of motorways, banks, electricity supply, etc.);
- promoting small-scale, labour-intensive industries, especially in rural areas;
- dispersing industrial development around the country and away from the main parts and Lagos;
- 'Nigerianising' industry so that Nigerians own industries or have a say in their running.

INTERNATIONAL DEBT

Many **developing countries**, especially those in South America and Africa, have a growing debt crisis (Fig. I.12). During the 1970s these countries borrowed money to aid their economic development from governments and banks in the industrial, **developed countries**. Meeting the interest and capital payments on this lending has become a real 'millstone' on the economies of these countries. The only way they can generate enough foreign currency to repay the debt is by boosting exports and cutting imports. The only way to cut imports, so that exports exceed them and provide enough to pay the debt, is by squeezing all domestic spending, which depresses the whole economy. Riots in Caracas, Venezuela, were caused by the tough economic measures such as higher petrol prices taken by the government to help it meet its debt repayments. Living standards have fallen by over 2 per cent per annum in Brazil, Nigeria and the Philippines since 1980, and poverty in these already economically poor countries increased. The problem might be solved in various ways: for example, creditor countries writing-off the debt; arranging discounts such as 50 cents in the dollar on the debt to reduce it; debtor countries permanently defaulting on their payments.

◀ Aid ▶

INTRUSIVE VULCANICITY

Lava (molten rock or magma) is ejected into and hardens within crustal rocks as well as being ejected directly on to the surface through, for instance, eruptions from volcanic cones. The former process is known as *intrusive* vulcanicity, the latter as *extrusive*. Intrusive vulcanicity affects surface relief either by buckling upwards the surface above the intrusion or by eventually becoming exposed on the surface after long periods of **erosion** of the overlying rock.

84

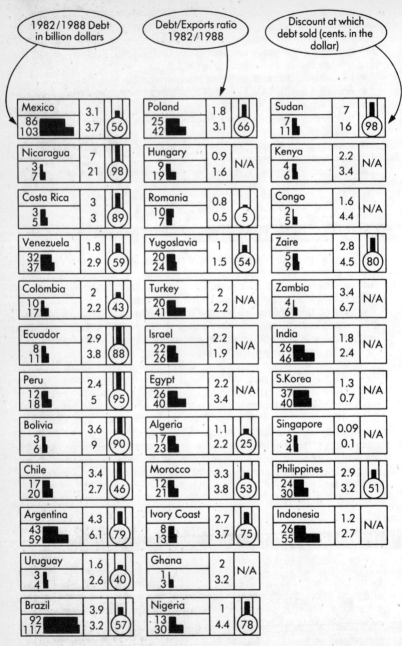

1982/1988 Debt in billion dollars			Debt/Exports ratio 1982/1988			Discount at which debt sold (cents. in the dollar)		

Mexico	3.1		Poland	1.8		Sudan	7	
86 103	3.7	56	25 42	3.1	66	7 11	16	98

Nicaragua	7		Hungary	0.9		Kenya	2.2	
3 7	21	98	9 19	1.6	N/A	4 6	3.4	N/A

Costa Rica	3		Romania	0.8		Congo	1.6	
3 5	3	89	10 7	0.5	5	2 5	4.4	N/A

Venezuela	1.8		Yugoslavia	1		Zaire	2.8	
32 37	2.9	59	20 24	1.5	54	5 9	4.5	80

Colombia	2		Turkey	2		Zambia	3.4	
10 17	2.2	43	20 41	2.2	N/A	4 6	6.7	N/A

Ecuador	2.9		Israel	2.2		India	1.8	
8 11	3.8	88	22 26	1.9	N/A	26 46	2.4	N/A

Peru	2.4		Egypt	2.2		S.Korea	1.3	
12 18	5	95	26 40	3.4	N/A	37 40	0.7	N/A

Bolivia	3.6		Algeria	1.1		Singapore	0.09	
3 6	9	90	17 23	2.2	25	3 4	0.1	N/A

Chile	3.4		Morocco	3.3		Philippines	2.9	
17 20	2.7	46	12 21	3.8	53	24 30	3.2	51

Argentina	4.3		Ivory Coast	2.7		Indonesia	1.2	
43 59	6.1	79	8 13	3.7	75	26 55	2.7	N/A

Uruguay	1.6		Ghana	2	
3 4	2.6	40	1 3	3.2	N/A

Brazil	3.9		Nigeria	1	
92 117	3.2	57	13 30	4.4	78

Fig. I.12 The world's debtor countries

Various intrusive features – a dyke, sill, batholith and lacolith – are shown in Fig. I.13. The name given to the intrusion depends on its shape, size and direction.

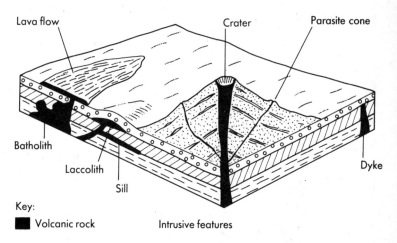

Fig. I.13 Intrusive and extrusive features

IRRIGATION

The watering of land by people rather than by precipitation (mainly rainfall) is described as irrigation. Areas that have insufficient water naturally for productive agriculture, principally the arid and semi-arid areas of the world, have long attempted to irrigate land. For thousands of years the River Nile has been used as a source of irrigating water by farmers in Egypt. Many farmers in Britain irrigate their fields in summer. The Central Valley Project in California (Fig. I.14) is a year-round irrigation and water control scheme which has enabled the area to become the most productive market gardening (truck farming) area in the world despite its very dry Mediterranean climate.

ISOPLETHS

Together with **chloropleths**, isopleths make up the main groups of maps. On isopleths, quantities are indicated by lines of equal value, such as contours (equal height above sea level) and isotherms (equal shade temperature). The contour map is perhaps the most common example, though isopleth maps are used to show climatic distributions (e.g., isotherms, isobars, isohyets) and changes in costs and profits over an area. Drawing an isopleth from a series of plotted points on a map requires care and thought if it is to have a fair degree of accuracy and also show the general distribution pattern.

Station	Annual rainfall (mm)	April–September rainfall (mm)
Fresno	149	20
Sacramento	471	58
Redding	663	92
Tahoe	2429	1010

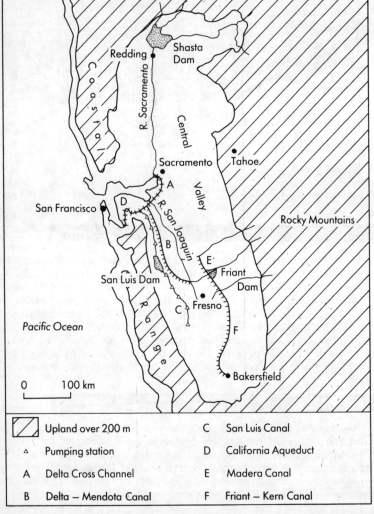

Fig. 1.14 The workings of the Central Valley Project, California

Fig. I.15 shows isohyets (lines joining places of equ...
drainage basin drawn from a series of point values.

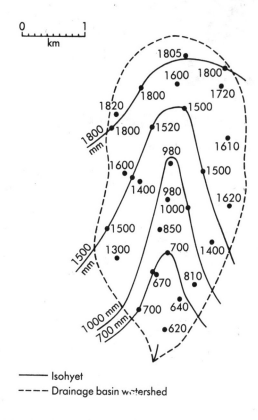

———— Isohyet
– – – – Drainage basin watershed

Fig. I.15 Isopleth showing isohyets

KARST SCENERY

Carboniferous limestone is associated with a very distinctive landscape and set of landforms. Surface drainage is lacking, with most of the drainage by underground streams, and many solutional landforms, such as swallow holes and caverns, exist. The term comes from the carboniferous limestone region of northern Yugoslavia named the Karst. In Britain, carboniferous limestone is found in the Pennines.

The physical properties of limestone, the fact that it dissolves in rainwater which is weakly acidic, lead to the development of the typical karstic features shown in Fig. K.1. The surface of carboniferous limestone areas has thin soils,

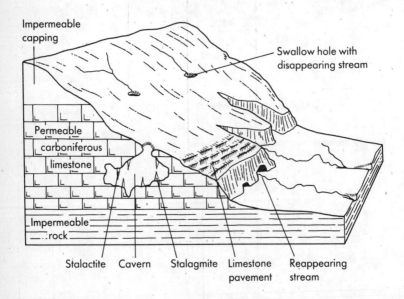

Impermeable capping

Swallow hole with disappearing stream

Permeable carboniferous limestone

Impermeable rock

Stalactite   Cavern   Stalagmite   Limestone pavement   Reappearing stream

Fig. K.1 Typical karst features

large amounts of bare, exposed rock and scree slopes with their fragments of broken rock. Vegetation is generally scanty. Underground features are common because of the rock's permeability; it has cracks and joints through which water passes. Well-jointed rocks are described as *pervious*. The Yugoslavian Karst region has developed features such as large openings in the rock called *poljes*, which are not found in this country. The lack of surface drainage, the upland nature and the poor soils of karst areas limit their human development. Limestone quarrying and the tourist potential of limestone areas are the exceptions.

The question of whether limestone quarrying should be permitted in a National Park is an interesting area of human conflict; people have different interests and attitudes here.

LAND RECLAMATION

The size of the Netherlands has increased over the past 150 years as a result of land reclamation. (See the table below.)

Land has been reclaimed from under the sea, the reclaimed areas beings known as polders. Dykes like the Barrier Dam across the entrance to the Ijsselmeer keep the sea from flooding polderland which is below sea level (Fig. L.1).

Polderland is used in a variety of ways, agricultural, urban and industrial. Arable farming yields per acre on the Ijsselmeer polders are among the highest in the world.

Year	Area (sq km)
1830	31, 500
1900	32, 000
1970	34, 000

LAND REFORM

Changing the ownership and arrangement of land may be necessary for the future success of farming in an area. For example, a large estate (e.g., a latifundium in southern Italy or Brazil), originally owned by absentee landlords living comfortably elsewhere and worked by tenant farmers, might now have been redistributed so that land is owned by the farmers themselves.

Latifundia in Brazil are usually either cattle ranches or coffee, cocoa or sugar plantations; their reform in many cases aids agricultural development. A fairer ownership of land tends to raise agricultural output.

Land reform schemes can involve changing both the tenure (e.g., breaking up large estates owned by landlords into smaller holdings owned by small farmers, as has happened in Kenya) and the arrangement of a farmer's holdings. Scattered plots have been consolidated into larger fields in parts of France in recent times, as they were during the enclosure movement in Britain nearly 200 years ago.

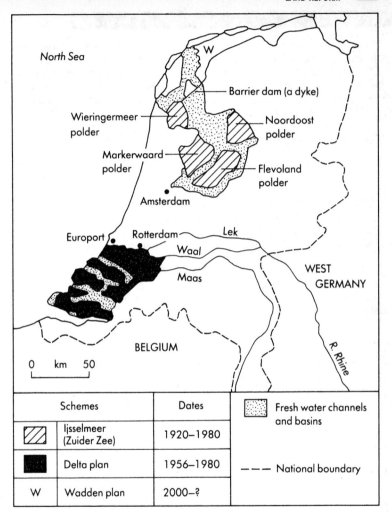

Schemes		Dates
▨	ljsselmeer (Zuider Zee)	1920–1980
■	Delta plan	1956–1980
W	Wadden plan	2000–?

Fresh water channels and basins

--- National boundary

Benefits of Ijsselmeer	Drawbacks of Ijsselmeer
■ more land for farming	■ expensive engineering involved
■ lake for freshwater and recreation	■ treatment necessary before land productive
■ sea flooding avoided	■ Amsterdam has declined as port

Fig. L.1 Land reclamation in the Netherlands

LAPSE RATE

Temperatures generally fall with altitude (height) in the lower atmosphere (the *troposphere*), as Fig. L.2 shows. This rate of change (normally decrease) of temperature with height is known as the lapse rate, of which there are two, the *environmental* and the *adiabatic*. The environmental lapse rate, which is merely the gradient of temperature in the atmosphere, averages out at 0.6°C per 100 metres (temperatures fall by roughly 0.6°C every 100 metres up). The adiabatic lapse rate is more complicated: when an air bubble rises it will generally cool as the atmospheric pressure around it falls; its rate of cooling is known as the adiabatic lapse rate. By comparing the environmental and adiabatic lapse rates in the atmosphere it is possible to say whether the atmosphere is unstable: in a stable atmosphere air pushed upwards at the surface will sink back so clouds will be rare; in an unstable atmosphere the air will continue to uplift, and clouds and rain are likely.

Lapse rates in the lower atmosphere normally show temperature falling with height. The atmosphere is heated not from above but from below by convection from the Earth's surface. The direct source of heat for the air is terrestrial rather than solar radiation. Gravity also means that atmospheric pressure declines with height; there is simply less air to be heated up at altitude and, therefore, it is cooler. An experiment with a bicycle pump on your finger soon shows that to increase the pressure is to increase the temperature (an adiabatic process).

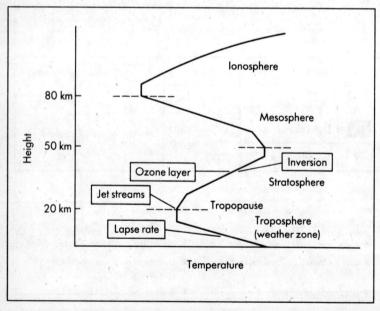

Fig. L.2 The effect of altitude on temperature in the atmosphere

LAVA FLOW

Basic lava can well out of a fissure in the Earth's crust and flow freely and rapidly for several miles before solidifying. Such an eruption would be quiet and may lead to the formation of a lava plateau. The Antrim lava plateau in Ireland is 1,500 square miles in area. Lava flows can also occur from volcanic cones usually shield cones composed of basic lava. Fig. L.3 shows lava flows in Hawaii, where flow speeds between 10 and 50 miles per hour are usual.

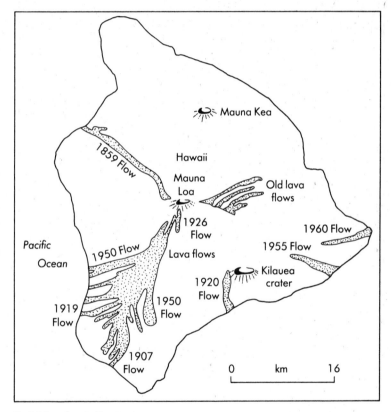

Fig. L.3 Lava flows in Hawaii

LEISURE

Leisure and tourism are at present the biggest growth industries in Britain. They are very labour-intensive, employing directly and indirectly 1.5 million people in hotels, restaurants, travel, transport and leisure activities. The size of the workforce has been increased by 22 per cent during the past ten years and at present jobs are being created at the rate of 50,000 a year. The leisure and tourism industries contribute 3 – 4 per cent of the GNP and bring in billions of pounds in overseas earnings. They are London's second biggest

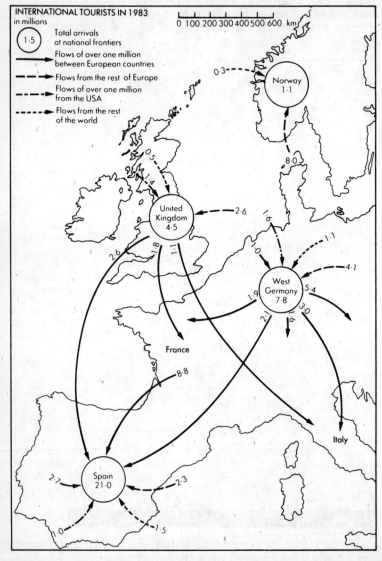

Fig. L.4

money-earner and since 1960 income from tourism has grown faster in Britain than in any other European country. Fig. L.4 shows European tourist traffic in 1983.

In today's recreation and leisure age, with its shorter working weeks, longer holidays and greater prosperity, facilities for recreation and leisure pursuits have developed in many areas. The table below shows three contrasting leisure activities in Rotherham.

Site	Location	Leisure activities
Herringthorpe Leisure Centre	Close to town centre with high accessibility on large open space	Athletics stadium; playing fields, including all-weather surface; tennis courts; swimming pool with wave machine, slide and large shallow water area and teaching pool; two 3-level sports halls for badminton, basketball, volleyball, indoor tennis, netball, cricket, five-a-side football, archery, rifle shooting, golf, fencing, martial arts, keep-fit and gymnasium activities. Suitable for public meetings, concerts, dances and exhibitions. Bar and restaurant. Community centre and sports centre
Ulley Reservoir	30-acre reservoir in a rural area outside built-up area	Sailing, canoeing, fishing and nature study on 20 acres of water.
Valley Park	70-acre park between two large housing developments in town suburbs	Tennis courts; bowling greens; putting green; pitch-and-putt course; landscaped and woodland footpaths

LIFE EXPECTANCY

In 1870 the expectation of life at birth for a baby boy in Britain was forty-one years and for a baby girl forty-five years; the figures are now seventy and seventy-six years respectively. Life expectancy, or the average length of an individual life, varies from time to time in the same community and from community to community at the same time. At the present time, the expectation of life at birth for baby boys and is seventy-two in Japan, seventy the USA, forty-two in Ghana and forty-one in India. There are old people in **developing countries** but in **developed countries** more people get through to seventy years, partly because *infant mortality* is far lower.

Infant mortality means the number of deaths before the age of one year, and can be expressed as a ration when compared to the number of live births. The infant mortality rates are approximately twenty per 1,000 in Japan and 100 per 1,000 in Mexico; in other words, 10 per cent of Mexican babies do not survive their first year of life! However, people aged fifty in developing countries such as India have almost the same life expectancy as people of fifty in developed countries. The difference between the two groups of countries is the percentage of people surviving to fifty; far fewer do so in developing countries.

Improvements in life expectancy are clearly going to be connected with improved health measures, housing, nutrition and other factors that reduce death. Improvements in medicine and health care (e.g., antibiotics, vaccines against particular diseases such as typhoid, better surgery, etc.) and in general living standards have been responsible for lowering infant mortality and raising life expectancy. Both of these do, however, vary between areas in a developed country; infant mortality is higher and life expectancy lower in the inner areas of large British cities than in the more prosperous, outer suburbs.

◀ Ageing population, Population explosion ▶

LOCALISATION

◀ Agglomeration ▶

LOCATION QUOTIENT

◀ Agglomeration ▶

LOAD

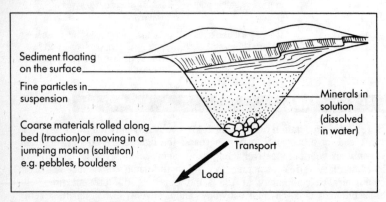

Fig. L.5 How material is transported

Rivers transport particles of rock material. This transported material is referred to as the river's load. The size of the load ranges from large boulders to very fine sediment. Generally, the size of the material carried decreases downstream.

In a river the processes at work which transport material include suspension, solution, traction and saltation (Fig. L.5). When the carried material comes into contact with the bed of the river channel it becomes known as *bedload*. Traction (rolling) and saltation (jumping) are bedload processes. Suspension and solution load is the carrying of lighter material by the running water and accounts for between 70 and 90 per cent of a river's total load. As Fig. L.6 shows, suspension load increases rapidly as the discharge of a river rises.

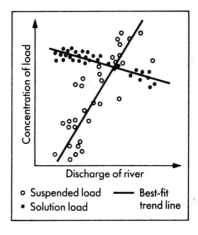

Fig. L.6 The correlation between load and river discharge

LONGSHORE DRIFT

This is the name for the process by which beach material is moved along a coastline by the waves (Fig. L.7). Along the south coast of England the most frequent winds are south-westerly. The result is a general movement of eroded material along the coast from Cornwall eastwards. When waves

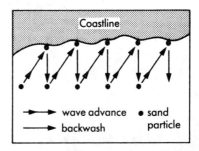

Fig. L.7 The process of longshore drift

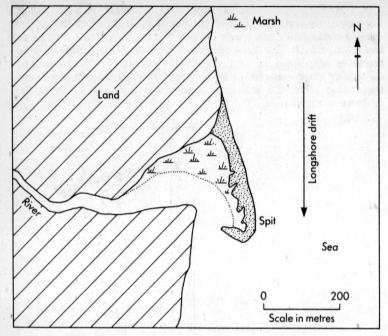

Fig. L.8 How longshore drift forms a spit

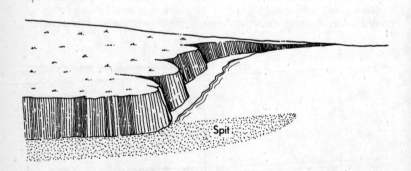

Fig. L.9 What the coastline will look like

advance at an angle to the coastline, material is moved along the shore, because the backwash will be down the gradient of the beach at right angles to the shore.

Groynes are constructed on beaches in an attempt to stop beaches being moved along the coastline by longshore drift. Where there is little or no attempt to halt this drift and where coastlines experiencing longshore drift change direction, various depositional features can form. Spits are an example (Figs. L.8 and L.9). A spit is a long narrow ridge of sand or shingle projecting into the sea and connected to the land at one end. Fig. L.10 shows the spit at

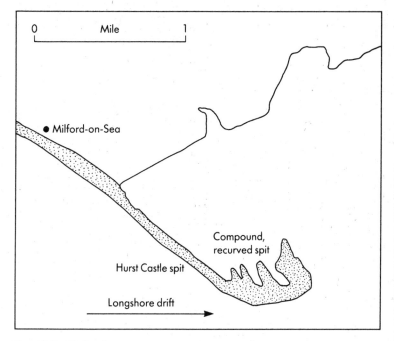

Fig. L.10 Hurst Castle spit

Hurst Castle near Milford-on-Sea, Hampshire, which is a compound, recurved spit. You will see that its end has been curved or deflected more than once by waves and currents. At Orford Ness on the East Anglian coast a spit has grown parallel to the coast and diverted the mouth of the River Orford. Chesil Beach near Weymouth (Fig. L.11) is a *tombolo*, that is, a shingle spit which has developed to join the mainland of Dorset to an offshore island, the Isle of Portland.

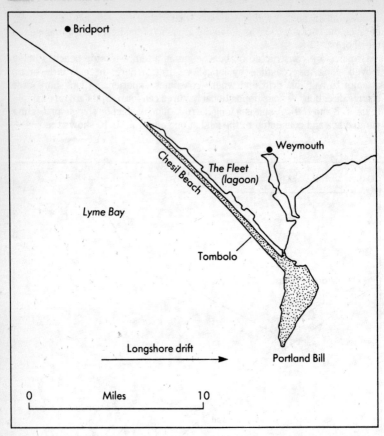

Fig. L.11 Chesil Beach

MARKETS

Distance from farm to market has a strong influence on what farmers decide to produce and can lead to the kind of land use pattern around large towns and cities shown in Fig. M.1. Close to large markets, market gardens producing fruit and vegetables and dairy farms producing fresh milk are often found. Further from the market, farmers may specialise in **arable farming** and livestock rearing.

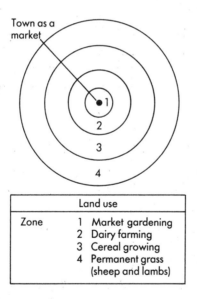

Town as a market

1
2
3
4

Land use		
Zone	1	Market gardening
	2	Dairy farming
	3	Cereal growing
	4	Permanent grass (sheep and lambs)

Fig. M.1 Land use around urban areas

Fig. M.2 helps to explain this pattern. Market gardening and dairy farming are examples of intensive farming on land with a high value in and close to the city. Vegetables and milk are bulky and perishable, and rapid, low-cost transport is required. Market gardens and dairy farms are usually very near major roads and railways to the large towns and cities. At about 8 km from the city centre, there is a change from dairy farms to wheat fields. Away from the market, arable and livestock farming become the more profitable. The lower land values make extensive farming possible. Wheat and beef are less perishable products so speed of transport to market is less important. The high transport costs to market faced by beef farmers can be covered by the higher prices that meat fetches.

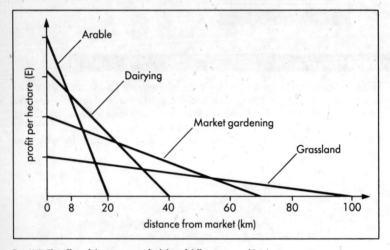

Fig. M.2 The effect of distance on profitability of different types of land use

The principle that farmland use, transport and distance to market are closely linked is important. It is a part explanation of land-use patterns on a number of different scales.

The intensity with which the land is used around many villages in West Africa decreases with distance from the village (Fig. M.3). A similar pattern can be seen on individual farms in Britain and on a much larger, national scale. The pattern of farming in Uruguay (Fig. M.4) resembles quite closely the pattern shown in Fig. M.1. Market gardening is based around Montevideo, where approximately 39 per cent of Uruguay's population live. Dairying followed by cereals or stock raising is the pattern in most directions from this zone of market gardening.

As many factors influence a farmer's decision, this pattern does not occur everywhere. For example, land use in the East Anglia area is not confined to intensive market gardening for the London market, because there are many different types of soil found there, some more suited to other uses. Improvements in transport can be another factor which changes the pattern. An effect of modern transport, for example, has been to move the boundary of the various zones further away from the market. In Britain in 1800 most market gardens and dairy farms were no more than a few kilometres from their market; now the situation is greatly changed.

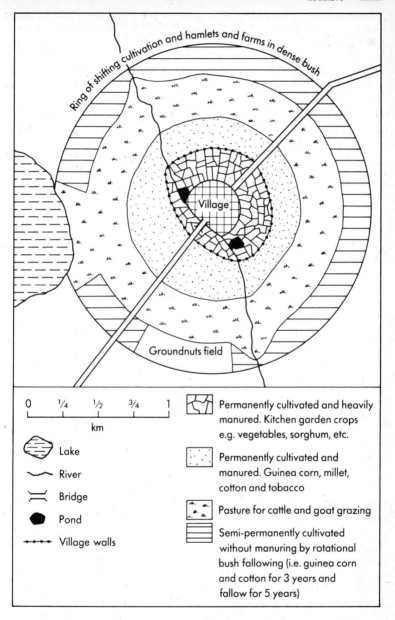

Fig. M.3 Farmland use around a village in northern Nigeria

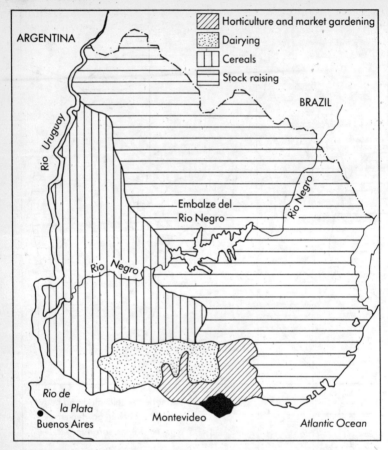

Fig. M.4 Farming pattern in Uruguay

MASS MOVEMENT

The term mass movement refers to the movement downslope, under the influence of gravity, of loose materials produced by rock weathering. Movement is not due directly to moving forces like rivers, ice and the sea. It is believed that mass movement of some kind takes place on all slopes with an angle of more than 5° and that this is the most important process of landscape change in Britain today.

There are four types of mass movement, some involving movement and landscape change at a very slow pace, often too slow to observe directly, and others with rapid movement. Material can move downslope by creeping, by sliding, by flowing and by falling (or by a combination of these). Soil creep leading to the formation of terracettes is one common type of mass movement (Fig. M.5). The material involved in soil creep is generally fine and moist, and the process tends to be slow but fairly continuous.

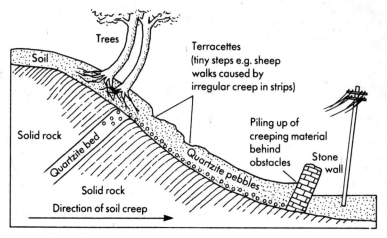

Fig. M.5 Soil creep leading to the formation of terracettes

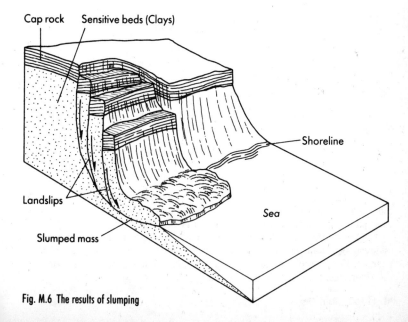

Fig. M.6 The results of slumping

Slumping due to sliding and/or flowing occurs along stretches of the British coast (e.g., Charmouth, Dorset). Slumping is a fairly rapid form of mass movement which occurs intermittently rather than continuously. Weather factors such as heavy rainfall and a difference between the loose material and the bedrock often have a major influence on the occurrence of slumping. The slumped mass and landslipping along a cliffed coastline shown in Fig. M.6 suggest that whole sections of clay have become detached from the cliff and have slid downhill in slabs, perhaps slowly.

MEANDERS

Many rivers have channels which swing (meander) across the landscape. The extent to which a channel meanders can be measured by calculating its *sinuosity*. This is done by comparing the overall length from source to mouth as a straight line with the overall length of the actual channel (Fig. M.7). The width across the valley floor which is occupied by a series of meanders is known as the meander belt (Fig. M.8).

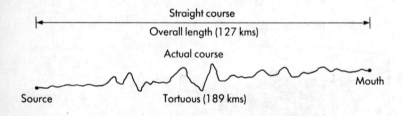

Fig. M.7 How to calculate the sinuosity of a meander

Why rivers meander, usually in their lower courses, is complicated and there is no clear and satisfactory explanation. It is not because of obstacles in their paths, nor because they are flowing more slowly (Fig. M.9).

It is known that meanders migrate, moving both downstream and laterally (sideways). When they migrate, they leave behind evidence of their former position. For example, swales are hollows of fine sediment which were once in the river channel.

◀ Flood plain ▶

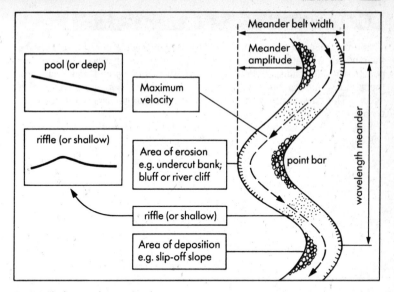

Fig. M.8 The features of a meander

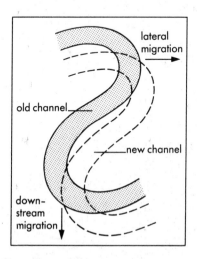

Fig. M.9 Block diagram of the lower course of a river valley

MIGRATION

This term refers to the permanent movement of people in order to relocate their home. Migration is one of the two basic ways in which the size of a population can change. When the numbers of immigrants and emigrants (people moving in and people leaving) do not balance, population change can occur. (The other form of change is natural population change, the result of changes in the birth and death rates).

Figs. M.10, M.11 and M.12 show three types of migration each of which will change as a country develops economically.

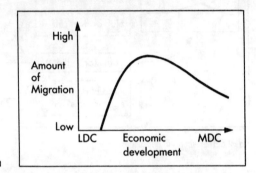

Fig. M.10 International migration

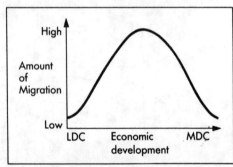

Fig. M.11 Rural-to-urban migration

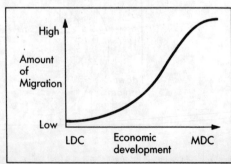

Fig. M.12 Urban-to-urban migration

Rural-to-urban migration is a common feature of many **developing countries**. Many villagers' solution to rural poverty is to leave for the towns and cities. Urban areas seem to hold the promise of success. Migration everywhere, domestic or international, is generally the result of a wish to improve living standards. Religious persecution and lack of political freedom are motives for migration but, generally speaking, the economic motive remains the strongest. The reasons for migrating and the obstacles to movement can be presented as a push-pull model (Fig. M.13). In the case of

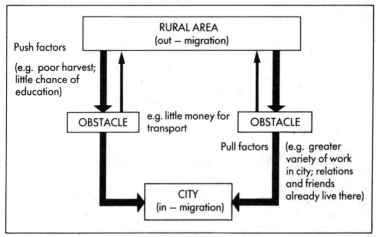

Fig. M.13 A rural-to-urban migration model

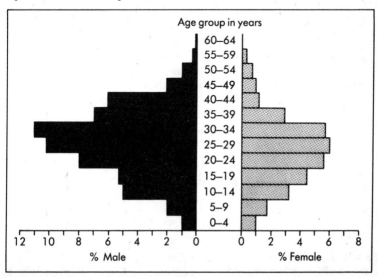

Fig. M.14 Population pyramid: migrants into Calcutta

rural-to-urban migration some factors push people out of the countryside, others act as a magnet and pull them towards the city.

Migrating populations are generally dominated by young and middle-aged males. The population pyramid showing migrants from the Indian countryside entering Calcutta reveals this pattern (Fig. M.14). Rural areas lose some of their most productive male workers.

Domestic migration in developed countries is the exact reverse of that in developing countries. Britain's main cities have been losing their population and rural populations have been rising, as have those of medium-sized towns, especially market towns. The trend is a drift of population from city urban areas, especially London, to town and rural areas. There are a number of factors responsible for this: for example, the search for a more relaxed lifestyle in the countryside; better travel facilities making long-distance commuting possible; the increasing de-concentration of job opportunities away from the large cities, etc.

MILLION CITIES

Until the 1930s the world's very large cities, those with populations greater than 1 million, were largely confined to the developed world (North America, Europe including the USSR, and Australasia). Today, however, the populations of many developing countries are not only increasing rapidly but also becoming increasingly urbanised (Fig. M.15). There are now more million cities (i.e., cities where population exceeds 1 million) in the developing world than in the developed world (Fig. M.17). The ten fastest growing cities in the world are all located in developing countries (Fig. M.16). In many developing countries population is becoming so concentrated in certain urban areas, largely through rural-to-urban migration, that one (a primate city) or two (a binary urban pattern) cities have an undue proportion of the country's population. For example, roughly a third of the populations of Argentina and Chile live in Buenos Aires and Santiago respectively. Many of these rapidly

Bolivia	34%→36%
Ghana	36%→42%
Japan	76%→76%
Mali	17%→20%
U.S.A	74%→72%
United Kingdom	78%→75%
India	21%→30%
France	73%→72%
Philippines	32%→37%

Fig. M.15 Changes in the percentage of population living in urban areas in selected countries, 1980–87

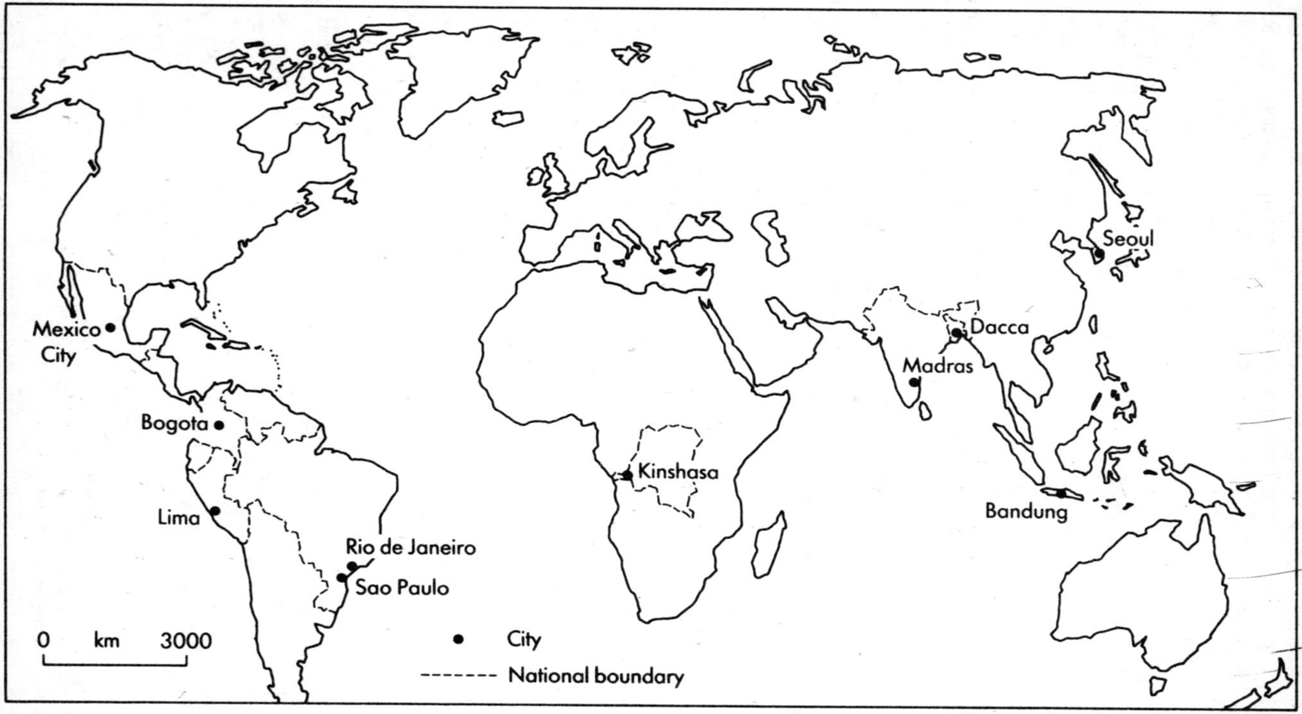

Fig. M.16 Location of the world's ten fastest growing cities

Mexico City

Bogota

Lima

Rio de Janeiro

Sao Paulo

Kinshasa

Madras

Dacca

Bandung

Seoul

0 km 3000

• City

------ National boundary

Region	Number of million cities			Million city population as a percentage of total population		
	1950	1970	1985	1950	1970	1985
Europe	28	36	40	15	19	20
North America	14	27	35	23	32	35
USSR	2	10	25	4	9	15
Oceania	2	2	3	24	27	34
East Asia	13	36	49	5	11	15
South Asia	8	27	48	2	6	8
Latin America	6	16	28	9	19	26
Africa	2	8	17	2	5	7
less-developed areas of the world	24	79	132	3	8	11
more-developed areas of the world	51	83	113	15	20	25
world total	75	162	245	7	12	14

Fig. M.17 Million cities, 1950–85

growing million cities in the developing world have **shanty towns**. Interestingly, million cities in the developed world tend to be losing population: London has lost, partly through urban-to-rural migration, about a quarter of its 1961 population.

MORAINE

◀ Boulder clay, Deposition ▶

MOTORWAYS

They are at the core of the modern road transport network, playing a major part in the reduction of time distances during recent years. The general location of motorways and major dual-carriageway roads is related to:
- the settlement hierarchy – motorways link large cities;
- relief – motorways and major surface transport routes are generally found on cheaper-to-build-on low, level land.

The choice of route for a new major road is often highly contentious; some people will be in favour of the route, others against it. The London Orbital motorway, the M25 (Fig. M.18) is more likely to be popular with firms in the outer London suburbs and people living in London streets once used by heavy lorries, etc. than with people living in houses now alongside its route.

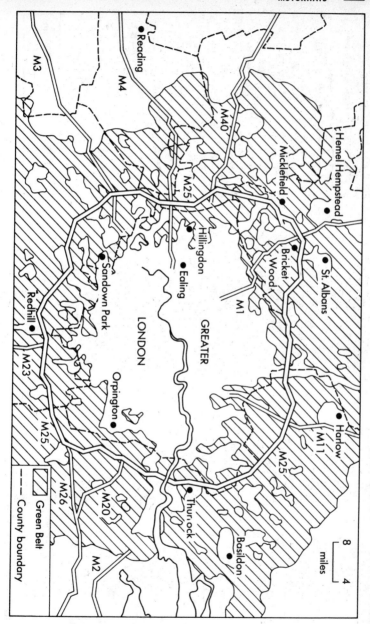

Fig. M.18 The route of the M25

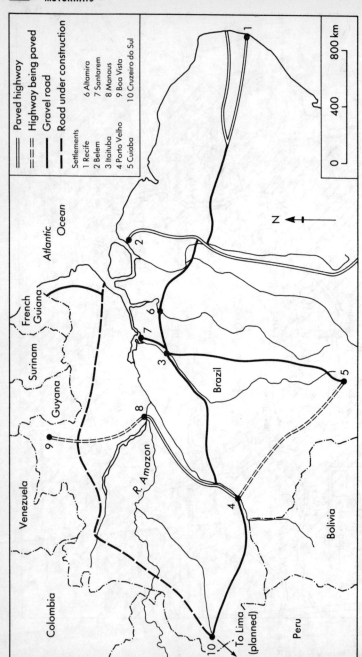

Fig. M.19 The Trans-Amazonian Highway

The Trans-Amazonian Highway (Fig. M.19) developed across the Amazon forest since the 1970s has its opponents (Fig. M.20), despite the fact that without it the economic development of the Amazon Basin would be very limited. The road has made it possible to transport minerals and other raw materials out of Amazonia and to bring in goods and supplies for new settlers.

◀ Distance ▶

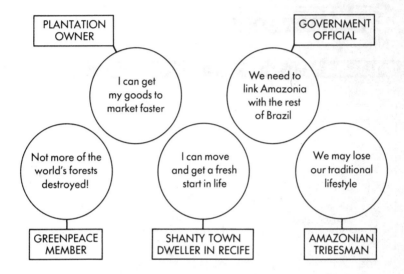

Fig. M.20 Arguments for and against the Trans-Amazonian Highway

NATIONAL PARKS

Fig. N.1 The ten National Parks of England and Wales

80 per cent of upland England and 30 per cent of upland Wales (land over 240 metres/800 feet high) has been designated as National Park (Fig. N.1) or as areas of outstanding natural beauty. Since the Second World War, the British countryside has been increasingly threatened by people's activities. Nature conservation and the protection of certain natural environments are now regarded as a responsibility of people; in National Parks *conservation* is a priority. However, this wish by many people to conserve parts of natural Britain can become a battle because other people may wish to use the land in other ways (Fig. N.2).

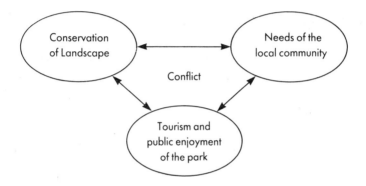

Fig. N.2 Sources of conflict in a National Park

One conflict of interest concerns the proposal of a mineral company to extend a limestone quarry at Eldon Hill in the Peak District National Park. The decision requires careful judgement, trying to balance all the issues. If it can be proved that the country needs the mineral and it cannot be obtained elsewhere, then permission to extend the quarry will be given.

Tourists themselves, growing in numbers thanks partly to the developing motorway network, are a source of conflict within National Parks. They create litter problems; the large numbers cause footpaths to erode; car parks, often 'eyesores', have to be built; narrow, country roads become congested with vehicles. The National Parks were set aside to preserve their special environment for people living in urban areas, yet the activities of these visitors can conflict with the National Park Authority and the interests of local people living in the National Park.

◀ Leisure ▶

NEW TOWNS

Most towns in Britain have developed slowly and naturally over the centuries. There are, however, towns which are generally all very modern, have grown from nothing very quickly and were planned on a drawing board before any building began; these are known as New Towns.

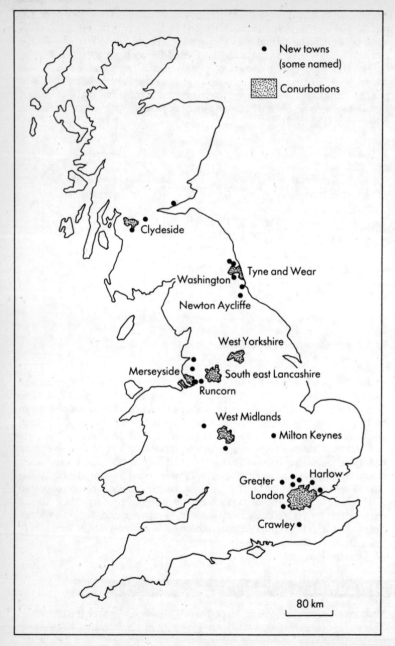

Fig. N.3 Map showing the position of conurbations and New Towns

They were designed to relieve problems occurring in old, well-established, large cities. Fig. N.3 suggests that many New Towns are overspill satellite towns for the very urbanised areas. Some have been built in the **Assisted Areas** of Britain as part of a government attempt to bring development to areas such as South Wales and Tyne and Wear.

The features of New Towns worthy of note are:

- the planners' desire to make the environment more pleasant for people living and working in New Towns is greater than it was in parts of the industrial conurbations. Industry and housing are not intermingled and that housing areas are surrounded by plenty of open space. Most New Towns are split into neighbourhood units; communities with their own shops and facilities within the town.
- most New Towns have a population with a young structure, younger than that of the country as a whole and that of most old established towns.

New Towns, with their planned layout, do occur outside Britain, including in the **developing world** (e.g., Malaysia).

NUCLEATED SETTLEMENT

Three types of settlement shape are recognised: *nucleated, linear* (or *ribbon*) and *dispersed*. Nucleated settlements have a distinct nucleus or centre: for example, they may have developed around a crossroads or market square. Linear settlements (Fig. N.4) show ribbon development, usually along a road, and are long, narrow settlements. Parts of a nucleated settlement may also show ribbon development as the place has grown out alongside a major road. The plan of the nucleated English village in Fig. N.5 also shows elements of dispersion around the edges of the village. Truly dispersed settlements are scattered and widespread, with much open space and undeveloped land within the settlement boundary.

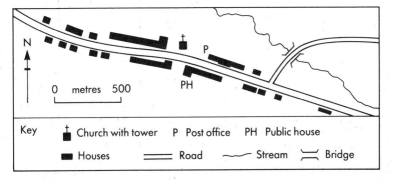

Fig. N.4 A linear settlement

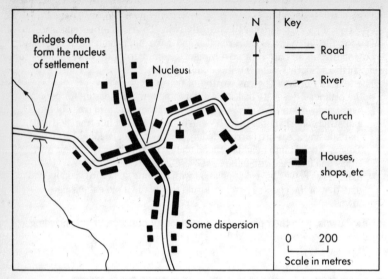

Fig. N.5 A nucleated settlement

OFFSHORE BAR

This is a ridge of sand, mud or shingle formed offshore, parallel to the coast. It is independent and not attached to the shore. It forms on gently sloping shorelines where waves break and, therefore, deposit material some distance offshore. Lagoons and marshes often develop between the bar and the shoreline, and waves tend to move the bar landwards. In-filling of the lagoon and drainage of the marsh may leave the bar as a line of dunes. Miami Beach, Florida, has developed in this way (Fig. O.1).

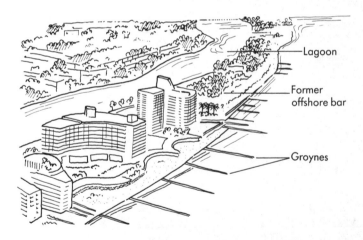

Fig. O.1 Miami Beach, Florida

ORDINARY BUSINESS DISTRICT (OBD)

There are usually about five shopping locations in a large city:
- in the city centre (**central business district**);
- in a superstore on the city outskirts;

- at a corner shop in either the inner or outer suburbs;
- at a neighbourhood shopping centre (a small parade of shops selling day-to-day needs, mainly convenience goods such as bread);
- in an OBD, a large suburban shopping centre.

These district shopping centres serve large districts of the city with a choice of convenience goods and a basic range of consumer goods and personal services. There will be only a small number of them in a city, and they are often found where roads from the city centre cross roads running across the city. They tend to be the old village centres overrun by **urban sprawl**. Between 100 and 250 shops may be available in an OBD, including a few chain stores (e.g., Boots the Chemist), several large supermarkets, several specialist shops (e.g., jewellery, shoes, carpets, dresses), some

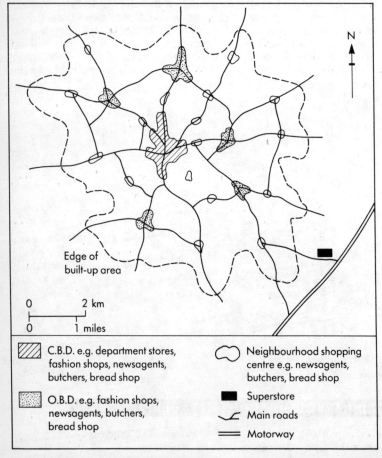

Fig. 0.2 Shopping areas in a city in the developed world

personal services (e.g., banks, building societies) and many everyday-need shops (e.g., baker, butcher).

These suburban high street shopping centres will have the largest trade area in the city apart from the CBD.

Fig. O.2 shows four types of shopping location and gives examples of the types of shop you might expect to find in each. The locations vary in the range and order of goods and services they sell: small neighbourhood centres provide a limited choice of low-order goods (everyday needs or convenience goods), whereas in the CBD there is choice and high-order goods (e.g., women's fashion clothes) are available.

OZONE LAYER

This is a layer in part of the upper atmosphere known as the *stratosphere* which is rich in ozone gas and where temperatures rise. This ozone is the Earth's natural shield against the sun's dangerous ultra-violet radiation. Holes in this ozone screen have been discovered by scientists above the Arctic and the Antarctic. This damage will let in more of the sun's rays, so contributing to the temperature rise known as the '**greenhouse effect**', as well as increasing the likelihood of skin cancer and premature ageing of people's skins. The depletion of the ozone layer seems to be caused by pollution, especially as a result of the increasing use of chemicals called chlorofluorocarbons (CFCs) in such items as refrigerators, foam packaging, aerosol sprays and industrial solvents. CFCs are also very efficient 'greenhouse' gases, contributing to the warming of the Earth by trapping in the lower atmosphere heat. They concentrate in the stratosphere, where they react with sunlight to produce chlorine, which attacks the ozone (Fig. O.3). Many people believe their use should be

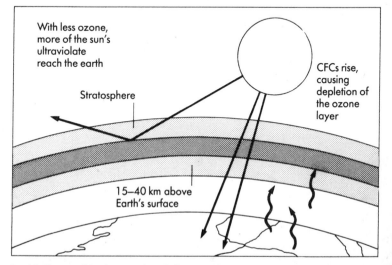

Fig. O.3 The ozone layer, how it works and what is going wrong

reduced; **developing countries** generally believe that the first step should be taken by the developed, industrial world.

◀ Deforestation ▶

PASTORAL FARMING

Farms can be classified as follows, according to the type of output they produce:
- arable – where farmers plough the land so that crops like grain and vegetables can be grown;
- pastoral – where farmers keep animals for either meat (e.g., beef cattle), milk (e.g., dairy cattle) or other products (e.g., wool);
- mixed – where farmers keep animals and grow crops in equal proportions

◀ Arable farming ▶

PERIGLACIAL AREAS

◀ Boulder clay ▶

PERMAFROST

◀ Boulder clay ▶

PERMEABILITY

Rock which allows water to pass through it is said to be permeable. Rock can be permeable either because it is pervious, like carboniferous limestone, that is, composed of large joints down which water can pass, or because it is porous, like chalk, which is composed of tiny air spaces which can fill with water.

Impermeable rock will not allow water to pass through it. Millstone grit is an example; as a result, it makes a suitable type of rock on which to construct reservoirs.

The permeability or impermeability of the rocks in the area will affect the level and amount of ground water (the area of saturated rock beneath the surface), whether drainage is on the surface or underground and whether springs occur or not. When ground water becomes trapped between two impermeable layers of rock and so cannot escape either upwards or

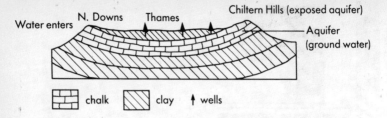

Fig. P.1 The London Basin

downwards, as is the case with the London Basin (Fig. P.1), an artesian well is produced as soon as a well is sunk through the upper layer of impermeable rock. Water reaches the surface by pressure of water itself: for example, many of central London's fountains operate this way. There is an artesian basin under part of the Sahara desert (Fig. P.2).

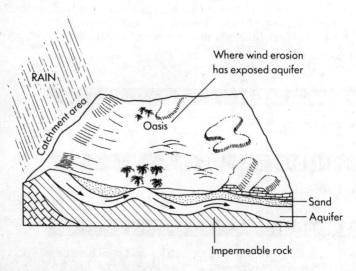

Fig. P.2 Oases in the Sahara Artesian Basin

PLANTATION

A plantation is a large farming estate, usually in tropical areas and owned by a company. There is large-scale production, often of a single crop (e.g., rubber, tea, sugar cane, cotton), principally for sale outside the area of production and for processing by the parent company. Plantations can be examples of extensive farming (they use large areas of land) and monoculture (specialisation in one type of output).

Dunlop rubber plantations in Malaysia are typically 4,000 hectares and employ around 200 full-time workers. Plantations are associated with the colonial era; they had European capital (money, equipment, etc.) and managers but local labour (e.g., rubber tappers). They were social communities, with people living on the estate.

Plantations have both advantages (e.g., they provide higher living standards for plantation workers and a guaranteed export market) and disadvantages (e.g., they do not provide local food supply and mean that the land is in foreign control) for the tropical countries concerned.

PLATE TECTONICS

It is now accepted that the Earth's crust is split into fourteen giant slabs, or rigid 'plates' of crust, which move in relation to one another. Interesting tectonic activity takes places at the boundaries of these moving plates, or plate margins, as they are known. The term *tectonic* refers to the forces which sculpt the Earth's surface from within the Earth; they are internal forces (e.g., mountains built by rocks being folded upwards; volcanic eruptions creating new land) rather than external forces working on the surface itself.

Plate margins move in three ways:

- they hit each other head-on (converge and collide). This is described as a *destructive* plate margin, because crust is likely to be lost as one of the plates is 'subducted' back into the Earth's molten mantle below and melts. The Nazca Plate under the Pacific Ocean and the American Plate forming the continent of South America meet and collide along the west coast of that continent (P.3).

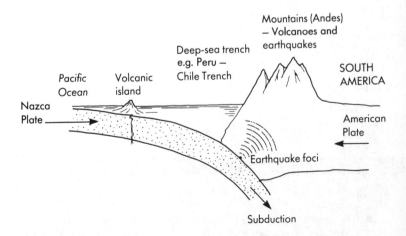

Fig. P.3 A destructive plate margin

- they pull apart (diverge). This is referred to as a *constructive* plate margin. New crust is created as ridges and volcanic islands are built as a result of lava welling through from the molten mantle below. When plates diverge under the ocean, as they do beneath the mid-Atlantic Ocean around Iceland, where the North American–Greenland Plate and the Eurasian Plate move apart, sea-floor spreading is said to take place. The Mid-Atlantic Ridge, a 2,500-metre-high mountain range rising from the bed of the Atlantic Ocean, has been built. Underwater volcanic eruptions, first noticed on 14 November 1963, had by February 1964 created the one-kilometre-square, 174-metre-high island of Surtsey, off the south coast of Iceland. It continued to grow at an equally rapid speed (Fig. P.4).

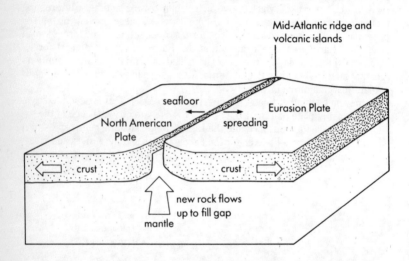

Fig. P.4 A constructive plate margin

- they glide past each other sideways. The sideways sliding of plates is the principal cause of major earthquakes. The San Andreas Fault in California provides a constant earthquake threat. The Pacific and North American Plates slide sideways past each other along this fault line (Fig. P.5).

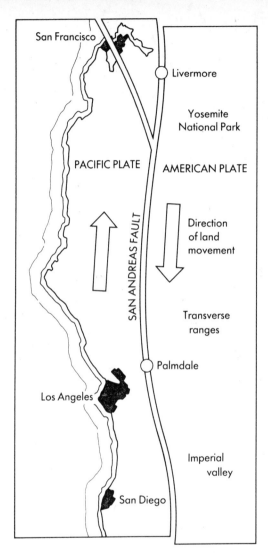

Fig. P.5 Sliding plates

Figs. P.6 and P.7 show both the major geological plates, their boundaries and their direction of movement and also the close association which exists between the location of these plate boundaries and the distribution of **earthquakes, fold mountains** and **volcanoes**.

Currently, Britain does not experience such tectonic activity and geological instability; it is safely located several hundred miles from the nearest plate edge.

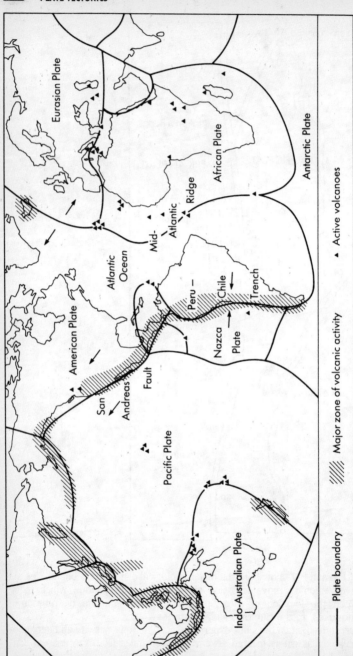

Fig. P.6 The correlation between plate boundaries and earthquakes, fold mountains and volcanoes

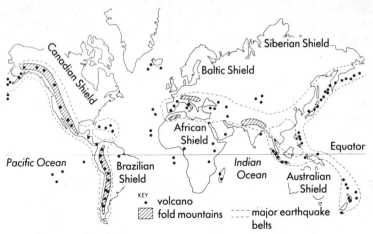

Fig. P.7 The major geological plates

POPULATION (DEMOGRAPHIC) TRANSITION MODEL

Demographers (students of human population) have noticed a pattern in the development of countries' populations: they appear to have developed through four basic stages. The population (demographic) transition model shows these stages, which are normally presented as in Fig. P.8. The model deals only

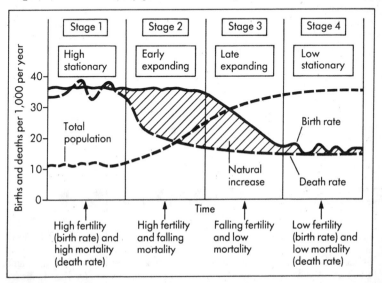

Fig. P.8

with natural population change, not with that resulting from migration of people. Natural increase results when the birth rate exceeds the death rate; natural decrease when the opposite happens.

The birth rate is defined as the number of live births per thousand people and the death rate as the number of deaths within a thousand of the population. Comparing the two rates will tell you whether the population of a thousand has grown or declined. Fig. P.8 shows period of little or no natural population change (the stationary stages 1 and 4) and of natural increase (the expanding stages 2 and 3). The world's **developed countries** tend to be in stage 4 at the present; many **developing countries** are in stages 2 and 3.

POPULATION DENSITY

This is a measure of the number of people living per unit area, normally per square kilometre. It is usually calculated for regions and countries, enabling regions and countries of different areal size to be compared. For example, there are more people in China than the Netherlands, but China is less densely populated.

The formula for measuring population density is:

$$\text{Population density} = \frac{\text{Population}}{\text{Area}}$$

The population densities of the five continents work out as follows: Europe 91, Asia 68, the Americas 11 and Australasia 2. These densities can be plotted on a map to show the world distribution of population. The world's population is not evenly distributed. There are areas where many live (termed popular areas) and areas where few live (sparsely populated areas with a **hostile environment**). We live in a world of conurbations at one extreme and deserts at the other! Contrary to popular opinion, very little of the Earth is densely populated or overpopulated; on the whole, it has a low population density and vast expanses are empty.

The population density of an area tends to reflects its economic potential for people, that is, the opportunities for food and water supply and for earning a living. **Relief**, climate, mineral deposits, **accessibility**, etc. all affect economic potential of a region. For example, people tend to live between 15 and 200 metres above sea level, close to exploitable sources of energy, and not in certain climates.

POPULATION EXPLOSION

This term is used by geographers to describe the massive increase in the number of people on the Earth over the past 150 to 200 years. Fig. P.9 shows that the curve 'rockets upwards' during this present century. It took until about 1830 for the first thousand million people to be on Earth at the same time; at present around five years is all it will take to add another thousand million (Fig. P.10)! The human population is snowballing!

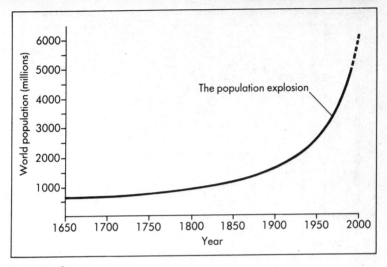

Fig. P.9 Population increase

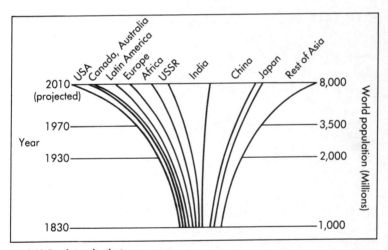

Fig. P.10 Population distribution

Only natural increases (births exceeding deaths) can be responsible for such global population increase. The basic cause is the declining death rate in **developing countries** (Fig. P.11). As Fig. P.12 indicates, it is in the countries of Africa, Latin America and especially Asia (e.g., Bangladesh, Mexico, Nigeria, etc.) that population increase is most rapid. The main cause of this is modern medicine. Parents in developing countries are not having

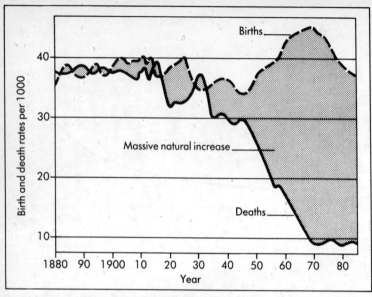

Fig P.11 Birth and death rate for Africa, Asia and Latin America

Country	1982 Population (millions)	Estimated 2050 Population (millions)	% Increase 1982–2050
Bangladesh	93	357	284
Brazil	127	279	120
China	1008	1450	44
India	717	1513	111
Indonesia	153	332	117
Mexico	73	182	149
Nigeria	91	471	418
Pakistan	87	302	247
USA	226	288	27
USSR	265	358	35

Fig. P.12 A comparison of population increase in developing and developed countries

more children than in the past; the birth rate has been fairly steady in these countries. However, more children born in these countries are surviving, thanks to medical, dietary, hygiene and sanitation improvements. Infant mortality rates have dropped. Developing countries tend to have very young population structures, with children forming a very high proportion of the population. For example, in India 49 per cent of the population is under twenty years of age.

Developing countries differ in their attitudes and reaction to the population explosion. Those who think it is a liability to their prosperity and development see the problem as the medievally high birth rate (a level of birth rate more appropriate to a medieval country, with its high death rate!). Bringing down the birth rate is the problem that these governments face. It is a very difficult task which has not met with a great deal of success generally. China embarked on perhaps the most ambitious campaign, with its one-child family policy, launched in 1980.

Changing people's attitudes, customs and habits is an enormous task. Most government efforts have involved education (e.g., family planning advertising campaigns) and most have generally been resisted by people. **Economic development** and rising living standards (e.g., greater educational and job opportunities for women) is likely to reduce the birth rate, but how does a country develop in the first place when population increase is hindering development?

◀ Ageing population, Life expectancy ▶

POPULATION PYRAMID

Data on age and sex structure of a population, can be presented as a diagram known as a population pyramid. The data for each age group of each sex are represented as horizontal bars. When all bars are completed for a more

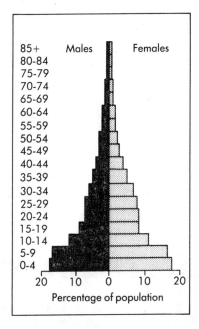

Fig. P.13 Population pyramid for Ghana (1980)

traditional society (e.g., nineteenth century Britain or a present-day developing country) the diagram has a pyramidical appearance as the length of the bars reduce upwards; in other words, the older the age group, the fewer there are of that age.

Fig. P.13 shows a pyramid: birth rates are high and life expectancy is not.

The typical pyramid for a developed country at present is not pyramid-shaped; it tends to resemble an onion instead! The lower birth rates and higher life expectancies are reflected in its population pyramid. Fig. P.14, the population pyramid for Britain in 1980, typifies the changes that have been taking place in most developed countries in recent times.

◀ Ageing population ▶

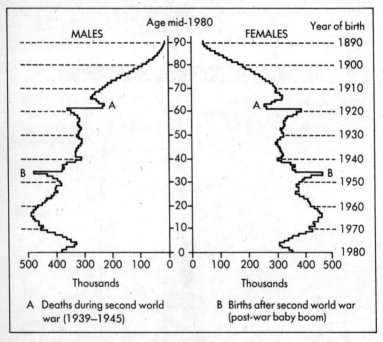

Fig. P.14 Population pyramid for the British Isles (1980)

PRECIPITATION

The term refers to all the moisture in its many forms (rain, snow, hail, mist, sleet, dew, fog and frost) that reaches the Earth's surface. Precipitation is caused by the cooling of air below its dewpoint temperature; this cooling is usually caused by the air's rising.

Rainfall is the most common form of precipitation and the most straightforward to measure. Snowflakes will fall if the air in the lower atmosphere and perhaps the ground too are close to freezing point. Sleet is snow which has partly melted during its descent from the **clouds**; the air is warmer than when snow falls. Fog is ground-level cloud formed by the cooling of air in the lower layers of the atmosphere. Radiation fog is a commoner type of fog in Britain; clear skies at night cause rapid cooling of the lower air and the condensation of its water vapour, provided the air is sufficiently moist.

◀ **Relative humidity** ▶

QUALITY OF LIFE

Every indicator of welfare and development has its shortcomings, and it is recognised that one cannot measure human welfare adequately using a single indicator. It is doubtful whether one can ever measure how happy people are.

In an attempt to put a value on the quality of ordinary people's lives, it is possible to calculate the Physical Quality of Life Index (PQLI) for a country from a range of the indicators of general social well-being for which figures are available.

Fig. Q.1 shows the level of some of these indicators for selected countries in 1986. The PQLIs shown are based on three of these indicators: the infant mortality rate, **life expectancy** and the basic literacy rate. This index is thought to give a clearer picture of how ordinary people's basic needs of life

Indicator	Country					
	Brazil	India	UK	Japan	USA	Kenya
life expectancy at birth (in years)	64	56	74	77	76	54
energy consumption per head (kg of oil equivalent)	753	187	3441	3135	7302	111
TV sets per 1000	118	2	430	390	476	1
adult literacy rate (%)	76	36	98	96	98	47
% of population living in urban areas	65	21	78	76	74	14
birth rate	38	43	12	25	13	49
GNP per head (US $)	1720	260	8570	10630	15390	310
number of people per doctor	3500	4795	800	898	645	7829

Fig. Q.1 A range of indicators for various countries from which to construct a PQLI are being met and whether general developments in industry and economic welfare actually benefit such people's lives. A quality of life gap between some **developing countries** becomes very noticeable, and the 'developed-developing' world gap is narrowed in some cases. However, it has to be remembered that many of these quality of life indicators have a strong relationship with GNP per head levels (Fig. Q.2). Industrial activity brings substantial improvements in both economic and total human welfare to countries and their individual citizens generally. All national welfare indicators hide pockets of poverty and prosperity within the country. The contrasts between regions and even within smaller areas like cities can be quite marked. Census data for UK cities illustrate this point.

Country	(0–100)	GNP per head, 1986 – US $
UK	96	8570
Sri lanka	83	360
India	43	260
Nigeria	25	730
Ethiopia	16	110

Fig. Q.2 The PQLI and GNP per head of five countries

RADIATION

Short-wave radiation from the sun heats the Earth's surface. Only about half of this incoming energy reaches the surface, as Fig. R.1 shows. The atmosphere is heated from below, with the greater part of the incoming solar

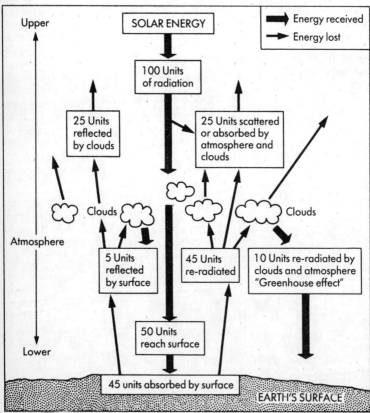

Fig. R.1

radiation passing down through the atmosphere unabsorbed. The energy reaching and absorbed by the Earth's surface is ultimately returned to space as reradiated long-wave terrestrial radiation. Long-wave radiation from the Earth heats the air above it by conduction.

This process of heating of the atmosphere helps to explain the **lapse rate** of temperature, why temperatures are lower at higher altitudes; and the rising and cooling of air leads to the condensation of water vapour and the formation of **clouds** and rain.

RAINFALL

Rainfall is the principal type of **precipitation**. It results from the rising and subsequent cooling of air. The air's ability to hold moisture depends chiefly on its temperature. When air cools, this ability falls, hence, condensation of the water vapour into clouds. Some clouds rain. The process by which rain is made in a cloud from the tiny water droplets which form the cloud is known as the *Bergeron Process*.

There are three ways in which air is forced to rise from the Earth's surface and so cool, leading to the development of rain clouds. The three types of rainfall are named after these three ways. First, *cyclonic* rainfall, which is associated with the passage of a **depression**. At the fronts (the boundaries between warm and cold airmasses) air moves upwards. Second, *convectional* rainfall, which is caused by the upward movement of air which has been heated by high surface temperatures. Warm air rises. The daily afternoon rainstorm along the Equator and summer thunderstorms associated with an **anticyclone** over Britain are examples of convectional rain. Third, *orographic* or *relief* rainfall: here, high relief pushes moving air upwards. The uplands of northern and western Britain owe their higher rainfalls to the relief factor. The explanations of relief rainfall and the rainshadow effect, which means that the leeward slopes of uplands receive large quantities of relief rain, are given in Fig. R.2. Fig. R.3 shows in cross-section the close relationship between **relief** and rainfall.

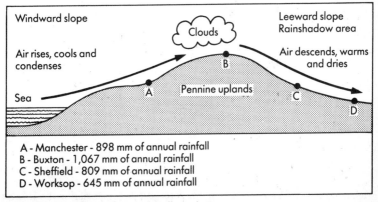

A - Manchester - 898 mm of annual rainfall
B - Buxton - 1,067 mm of annual rainfall
C - Sheffield - 809 mm of annual rainfall
D - Worksop - 645 mm of annual rainfall

Fig. R.2 Relief rainfall and the rainshadow effect in the Pennines

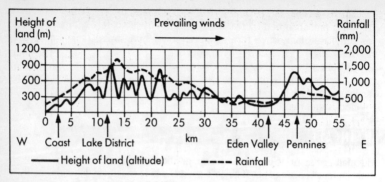

Fig. R.3 Cross-section of north-west England showing connection between relief and rainfall

RAISED BEACHES

The position of sea level in relation to land level is never fixed, at least not over long periods of time. Raised beaches are features that can be found along coastlines which are *emergent*, that is, the land level is rising in relation to sea level. They are usually wave-cut beach platforms covered with deposits of sand, pebble, etc. which now stand above the present sea level (Fig. R.4). They are the old, now dry coastline and may include dry caves, cliffs, etc. A rise in land level and/or a drop in sea level is responsible for their formation.

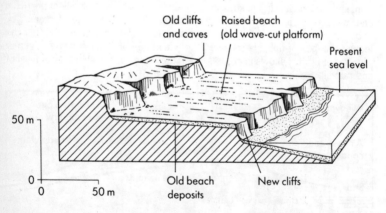

Fig. R.4

There are many examples of raised beaches around the Mediterranean coast (e.g., in Malta), representing periods in the past when the sea level was higher than it is today, such as warm, interglacial periods during the Ice Age when there was less ice in Europe than exists today.

RANGE

The range of a good or service is the maximum **distance** people will travel to buy or use it. Many goods and services are not provided in the settlements where people live, so travel may be necessary. Here are some approximate ranges for certain functions:

- Newsagent – 1 – 2 km
- General store – 2 km
- Butcher – 3 km
- Bank – 10 km
- Cinema – 20 km
- Superstore – 30 km
- Concert hall – 40 km
- University – 45 km

Note that the higher the order of the function, the greater its range.

Ranges can be shown on a map by drawing a line between a person's home and the furthest place they are prepared to travel for a particular good or service. These lines are known as *desire lines* and relate to one function only (Fig. R.5). Desire lines showing ranges of many separate functions can be used to determine a settlement's sphere of influence.

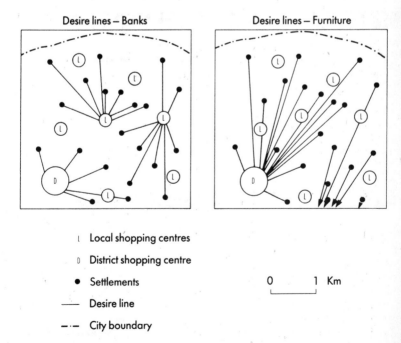

Desire lines – Banks   Desire lines – Furniture

l   Local shopping centres

D   District shopping centre

●   Settlements

0   1   Km

——   Desire line

–·–   City boundary

Fig. R.5 Desire lines for (left) banks and (right) furniture stores on the Isle of Anglesey, North Wales

RELATIONSHIPS

Relationships are cause-and-effect links or interactions, one factor acting upon another and perhaps vice versa. Geography is full of relationships. As a subject it is distinctive because it studies the relationships between people and the environment, especially the physical/natural environment. By environment is meant both the physical/natural environment (e.g., climate, relief, soils and vegetation, etc.) and the artificial, human elements of the environment (e.g., motorways, towns, conurbations, etc.)

People – environment relationships work in two ways: on the one hand, people are affected by their environment (e.g., by **earthquakes, hurricanes,** etc.) and on the other, they have the growing capacity to modify the environment, either deliberately or unintentionally (e.g., by the so-called **greenhouse effect**).

Many figures in this book show how two geographical factors are related. For example, there is a relationship between the size of a river's **load** and distance downstream from its source. However, it is important to remember that a statistical correlation between two factors is not necessarily a geographical relationship. It may be possible to correlate by statistical means crop yields in Brazil and the weather in Iceland; the two are extremely unlikely to be related in the real world!

RELATIVE HUMIDITY

This is a measure of the amount of moisture in the air. Measuring how wet the air is gives an indication of how likely **rainfall** is. Relative humidity is a ratio of the amount of water vapour the air can hold at that temperature. Relative humidities are expressed as percentages. A relative humidity of 100 per cent would indicate that the air is very wet (saturated); that it is at its *dewpoint temperature*. Very dry air usually has a relative humidity of around 50 per cent. Above 80 per cent the air has a distinct dampness, sultriness and closeness.

Humidity is measured by a hygrometer, with its wet- and dry-bulb thermometers, housed in a **Stevenson Screen**.

◀ Precipitation ▶

RELIEF

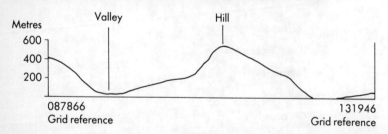

Fig. R.6

This is one of the core words in the language of the geographer. Relief refers to the shape and altitude (height) of the Earth's surface. Surface relief of an area is depicted by the contours (lines joining places of equal height above sea level) on an Ordnance Survey map. A cross-section can be drawn from contours to show the relief of the land along a line on the map (Fig. R.6).

RIA

Land and sea levels change over time. When sea levels rise relative to land levels either because of a rise in sea level or a drop in land level, the coastline is described as a *submergent* one.

It is believed that sea levels around Britain are currently rising because the Polar ice cap is slowly melting and putting more water into the oceans. The so-called **greenhouse effect** will merely add to an existing problem of land around the coast of Britain being drowned. The problem is made worse in south-east England because land is being tilted downwards into the sea by the upward recovery of Wales and northern Britain from ice which covered it during the Ice Age. It is slowly rising and causing the South and South-East to sink: London is thought to be sinking at the rate of about two feet a century – hence the Thames Barrier!

Flooded river valleys on the coast are known as rias. They are long, narrow, funnel-shaped inlets, common in Devon and Cornwall (e.g., Plymouth Sound, River Fal), south-west Ireland and north - west Spain.

RICHTER SCALE

◄ Earthquakes ►

RIFT VALLEY

Rift valleys, like **fold mountains**, **earthquakes** and **volcanoes**, tend to be found along definite lines of weakness on the Earth's surface. They are wide, flat-floored, steep-sided valleys formed by tectonic stresses in the rocks

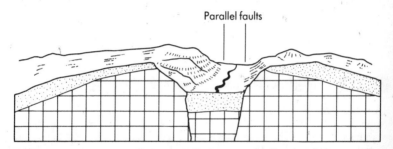

Parallel faults

Fig. R.7

around plate margins. If the great forces in the Earth's crust are pushing towards each other, rock breakage is likely. Two faults where the rock layer has broken will enable the two outer layers to thrust up over the centre layer. Sinking of the centre layer will produce a valley. Rift valleys can also be produced where parallel faults develop because the rocks are pulled apart and the central block between the two faults subsides (Fig. R.7).

The complex East African Rift Valley (Fig. R.8) system is the best example of a rift valley in the modern world. Rift valleys can be found in old volcanic but now geologically stable areas of the world (e.g., the Central Lowlands of Scotland, the Rhine Rift Valley of Germany).

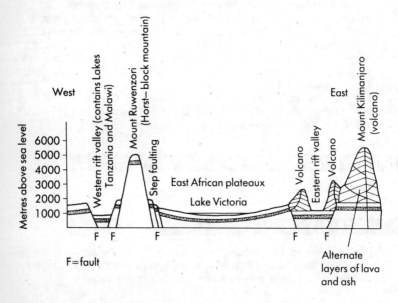

Fig. R.8 The East African Rift Valley system

RIVER CAPTURE

A very active river can erode backwards and extend its valley into the valley of a neighbouring river (Fig. R.9). This way the active river may 'capture' its neighbour's water. There are many examples of river capture: for example, in North Nottinghamshire the more powerful River Idle has 'beheaded' the original River Ryton at two points (Fig. R.10).

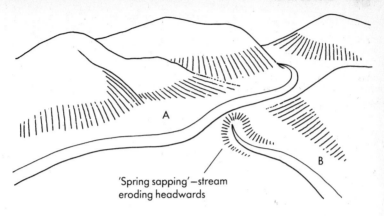

'Spring sapping'—stream
eroding headwards

By headward erosion, river B intercepts river A
and 'captures' its headwaters. B increases in size.
There is an abandoned section of A which is
reduced in size and becomes a misfit stream—
too small for the valley it occupies.

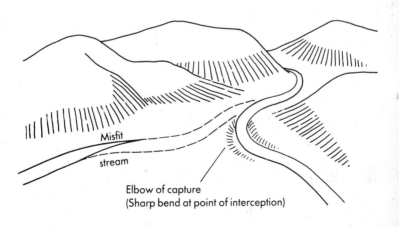

Misfit
stream

Elbow of capture
(Sharp bend at point of interception)

Fig. R.9 River capture

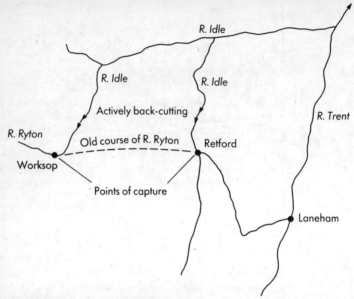

Fig. R.10 River capture in north Nottinghamshire

RIVER DISCHARGE

Rivers transport water. The amount of water in a river channel is referred to as its discharge (or streamflow). It can be measured for any river at any point of its course using the following formula:

Discharge = cross-sectional area of channel × velocity (speed) of water

Fig. R.11 shows this in operation.

Discharge normally increases downstream. The more channels a drainage basin has and the greater the area which feeds it, the larger the volume of

Measuring cross-sectional area (width x depth)

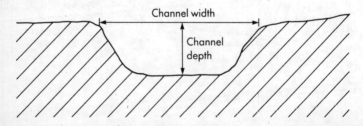

Fig. R.11 Measuring cross-sectional area of river

water one would expect to be in the river. The components of the water cycle will determine a river's discharge:

Discharge = precipitation − evapotranspiration ± changes in storage (e.g., infiltration into the soil)

RIVER MANAGEMENT SCHEMES

The water in most large rivers and large parts of their draining basins is managed and organised for the benefit of people: for instance, to ensure that safe water is available to large numbers of people for drinking and other personal uses.

An important river management scheme is the Tennessee Valley Authority Project, which has since 1933 sought to control and conserve the water and soil resources of the large basin of the River Tennessee, which covers seven states of the USA (Tennessee, North Carolina, South Carolina, Georgia, Alabama, Kentucky and Mississippi). In the 1920s this valley was typified by 'hillbilly' subsistence farming, large-scale soil erosion and regular flooding. Fig. R.12 shows how the project has helped to produce an enormous rise in the standard of living of people living in the Tennessee Valley.

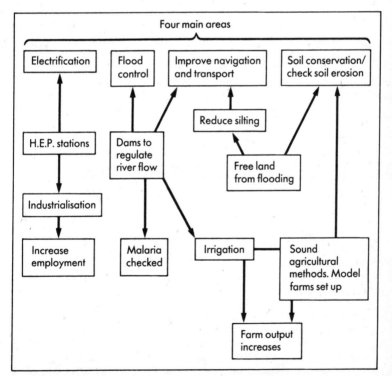

Fig. R.12 The Tennessee Valley Authority Project

In Britain, the Severn–Trent Water Company supplies an average of 420 million gallons of water a day to 8 million people through management of the Severn and Trent river basins, an area of over 8,000 square miles stretching from the Humber Estuary to the Bristol Channel, and from mid-Wales to the East Midlands. Supplying this water involves building and running reservoirs, water treatment works and sewage plants; laying and maintaining water mains and sewers; controlling the flow of the main rivers themselves; conserving the natural environment of the land in the basin, etc.

RIVER TERRACE

Terraces (flat stretches of land) can be found within river valleys. They are above the level of the river but roughly parallel with it, and made of alluvial (river-borne) deposits. They are the remains of an earlier **flood plain**, when the river's valley was at a higher level. A rise in land level or a drop in sea level has left the old flood plain high and dry above the new valley level. Much of central London is built on the river terraces of the Thames (Fig. R.13).

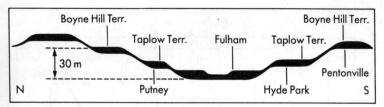

Fig. R.13 The Thames terraces

ROCK TYPES

Rocks are usually classified into three groups (Fig. R.14). First, *igneous* rocks: these include all those which have solidified from molten material (e.g., granite, basalt, dolerite). They tend to have a higher resistance to **erosion** (hard rock) and may be crystalline, especially if the cooling to solid rock was slow. Second, *sedimentary* rocks: these are composed of sediments either from the deposited broken material of other rocks (e.g., sandstone, millstone grit), from organic remains (e.g., coal, chalk, limestone) or from chemical processes (e.g., gypsum). Sedimentary rocks are less resistant to erosion (softer rock generally) and may have a fossil content, stratification planes (bedding planes) and joints. Third, *metamorphic* rocks: these were originally igneous or sedimentary but have been altered by either heat or pressure within the Earth's crust. Their character and appearance will have changed (e.g., metamorphosed limestone becomes marble, metamorphosed shale becomes slate). Metamorphic rocks generally have some resistance to erosion (tough rock) and form uplands.

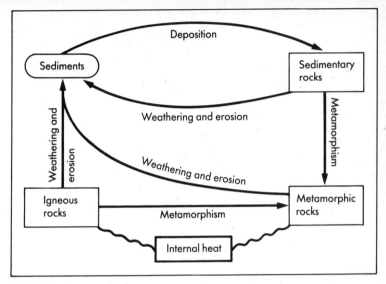

Fig. R.14 The three types of rock

RURAL LAND USE

Rural land used for farming can produce different kinds of food output. A range of factors might influence the land-use choice of a farmer (Figs. R.15 and R.16).

Farmers rarely have a free choice: only one type of farming might be possible because of physical factors the farmer can do little about, (e.g., the climate, the slope of the land, etc.). Factors influencing the farmer's decision as to how to use the land that cannot be changed or controlled are known as *constraints* on the decision. Economic and personal and social (human) factors

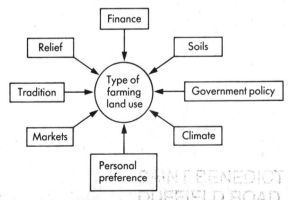

Fig. R.15 Factors affecting the farmer's land-use decision

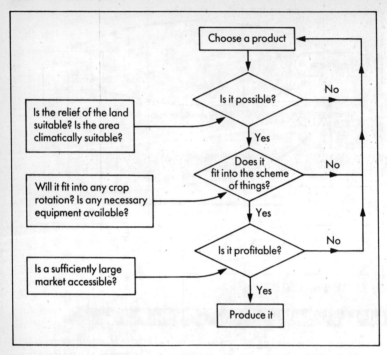

Fig. R.16 Deciding what to produce

are generally less likely to be constraints than environmental (physical) factors. For example, access to markets can be changed more easily than the climate and relief of an area.

The location of the customer (the market) is very important to certain types of farming (e.g., market gardening–the commercial growing of fruit, flowers and vegetables).

SAHEL

The term Sahel is derived from an Arabic word meaning edge or shore. It is now used with reference to countries such as Mali, Mauritania, Burkina Faso, Niger, Chad, Sudan, Ethiopia and Somalia which are on the southern edge of the Sahara Desert, where the rainfall and vegetation conditions are transitional between those of the true desert and those of the savanna (e.g., the Kenyan Game Parks).

These Sahelian countries have been a disaster area in recent years and are often referred to as the 'famine belt' of Africa, where hunger and absolute poverty have affected millions of people (Fig. S.1). A mixture of factors are to blame for this sub-Saharan crisis:

- rainfall has fallen in a rather on-and-off way since 1968, the year of the so-called Great Drought of Africa, and as a result harvests in the area have fallen by 15 per cent since then. The desert sands have expanded southwards and replaced the scattered shrubs and trees of some of the Sahel.

- annual population growth rates are among the highest in the world. The population of the Sahelian countries has doubled since 1968. Poor harvests and more mouths to feed have been causes of hunger and famine.

- civil wars (e.g., in Chad, Sudan and Ethiopia) have aggravated the problem. They have disrupted farming and caused depopulation of the countryside. People have felt safer in the towns, where they cannot farm! The urban population has been growing twice as fast as the rural population during the 1980s.

- corruption and poor food storage, marketing and distribution exist. Government administration of food prices and supply has often favoured the powerful groups in the cities and been designed to keep the peace there. Small farmers have often received low farm prices, which are a disincentive to farm. There has generally been inefficiency in farming and food supply in these countries, partly because of underinvestment in training people. For example, rats eat about a quarter of harvests and **deforestation**, which allows the soil to be eroded and the desert to grow further, has been permitted.

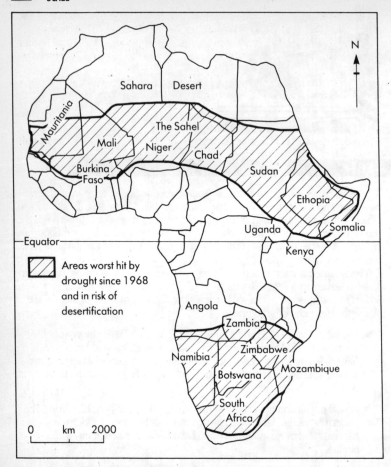

Fig. S.1 The Sahel and the drought in Africa

SCALE

The term scale is an essential part of the language of geography. It has two common uses. First, all accurately drawn maps have a scale shown either as a scale line or as a representative fraction (e.g., 1:25000). In the latter case the map is 25,000 times smaller than the real-world ground it represents.

Scale is also used to describe the size of the area being studied by geographers. Five scales are often recognised: *local* (a street, a village, a town); *regional* (a larger area such as a county or a region such as the East Midlands or the Punjab); *national* (the whole country); *international* (a number of countries or a large area of the world: (e.g., the European Community); and *global* (the whole world).

It is interesting how a change in the scale of study sees a change in the factors that are important in geography. For example, at local scale such factors as the aspect and slope of fields are important to an individual farmer whereas at the larger, national scale climate is important to farming generally.

SCATTERGRAPH

Scattergraphs are frequently used by geographers to graph two sets of data; the graphed points are left as a scatter of dots.

Fig. S.2 shows the Gross National Product (GNP) per head and adult literacy rates for seven countries.

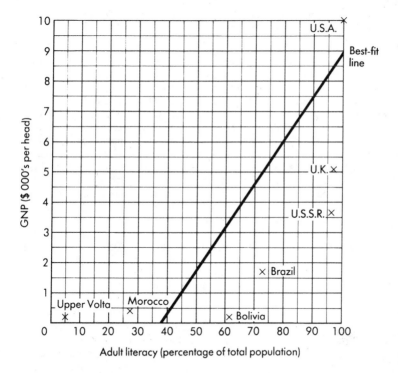

Fig. S.2 Adult literacy (percentage of total population) and GNP per head

Scattergraphs can be analysed to indicate the statistical relationship (correlation) that exists between the two sets of data graphed. A best-fit trend line needs to be drawn on the scattergraph and the line can be compared with the typical patterns shown in Fig. S.3.

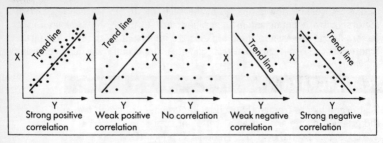

Fig. S.3 Typical patterns shown by scattergraph

SCIENCE (TECHNOLOGY) PARKS

The idea of industry and business being in a park-like setting has grown during recent years in **developed countries**. They are known by various names – business parks, research parks, technology parks, science parks office parks – and are most common in the USA. In Britain they are either on university sites (e.g., the Cambridge Science Park), in New Towns (e.g., Llantarnam Park, Cwmbran), in **Enterprise Zones** (e.g., Dundee Technology Park) or in a few forward-thinking towns and cities with access to airports and motorways (e.g., Bristol, Swindon, Birmingham, etc.). **High- tech industry** or 'sunrise' industry, producing computers, micro-electronics and telecommunication equipment and using techniques involving micro-electronics rather than old-style heavy manufacturing or low-tech industries, seems to be attracted to these parks. In these industries no special inputs or facilities are needed and neither the raw materials nor the finished products are bulky or heavy; they are 'footloose' and the availability of good modern transport facilities is important. Road and air are used to transport the small raw materials and products, and factories are usually single-storey, modern and may be automated. Studies in the USA show that high-tech industries are attracted to these industrial parks because:

- the immediate environment is of a high quality e.g., a pleasant environment of fully grown trees and lakes, attractively designed buildings with open spaces between them, plenty of facilities like restaurants, tennis courts, etc. They normally occupy a **'greenfield' site**, which will have a high amenity value (top-quality environment).
- they are close to universities and colleges, where there is expertise in science, computer research, etc. Industry and business working closely with university departments is a major feature of many industrial parks.
- they have been developed on sites with good communications (e.g., close to motorways and/or airports; helicopter pads, etc.)
- they can be close to other established high-tech firms. Links with other firms are seen as important.

One of the earliest, and now most famous, of British industrial parks is the Cambridge Science Park, opened in 1973 on 130 acres on the northern edge of the city, close to major roads. Sixty-eight science-based firms and research institutes have located in this attractive, well-landscaped park. It is developed to a very low density, with only about a sixth of the total area being building floor space. One condition of locating in the Park is that firms must be involved in the research and development of products rather than their large-scale manufacture, and must take advantage of links with the University. University-linked industry marrying scientific brains and business is the basis of the Science Park. Most firms are small and are mainly involved in laser, telecommunication, precision electronics and pharmaceutical production.

SEA DEFENCES

In some areas the sea is eroding away the cliffs; in others it is depositing material along the shore. The sea is eroding parts of the Yorkshire and Lincolnshire coastlines and building up stretches of the East Anglian and Lancashire coastlines.

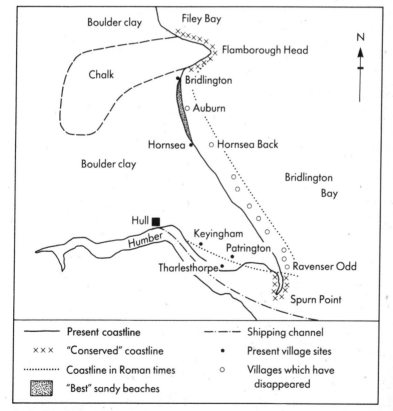

Fig. S.4 Map of the Yorkshire coast showing erosion

The sea pounds the bases of soft cliffs. In some places they are being eaten away at a rate of a few feet a year. The map of the Yorkshire coast (Fig. S.4) shows how villages and land have disappeared since Roman times along the softer **boulder clay** stretches.

In some areas where the cliffs are eroding quickly, huge sea walls have been built along their bases (Fig. S.5). Sometimes even these, built of thousands of tons of concrete, have been destroyed.

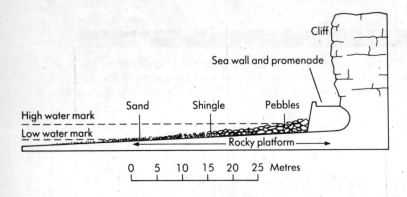

Fig. S.5 Sea wall along the base of a cliff

Sea defences are also constructed in order to prevent beaches from being washed away. Some seaside towns have built a series of groynes or breakwaters along the coast. They are usually made up of stout posts, connected together by sturdy railway-sleeper timbers. They stretch from high water mark down to the lower shore. The groynes are to prevent **longshore drift** eroding the beach. It is possible to work out the direction of longshore drift by looking at the different sand and shingle levels on either side of the groyne (Fig. S.6) – it may be a metre or so!

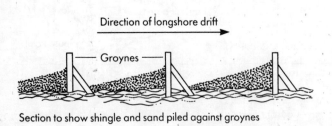

Section to show shingle and sand piled against groynes

Fig. S.6 Shingle and sand levels by groynes showing direction of longshore drift

Lyme Regis, Dorset, has a long history of using sea defences in an attempt to halt coastal erosion. Fig. S.7 shows recent proposals to improve the defence of the town's seafront. There is opposition to this plan by some residents of Lyme Regis, who claim it will ruin the character of the resort.

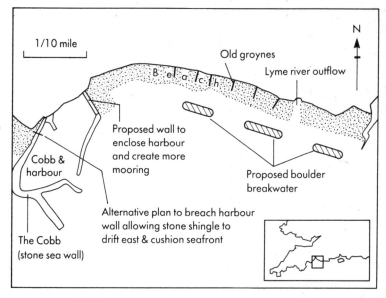

Fig. S.7 A proposal to defend Lyme Regis from further marine erosion, 1989

SECTORS OF INDUSTRY

The jobs or occupations in which people work are so numerous and varied that it is useful to group them. One system of classification in international use has nine groups:

- agriculture, forestry, hunting and fishing;
- mining and quarrying;
- manufacturing;
- building and construction;
- power and water services;
- commerce, insurance and banking;
- transportation, warehousing and communications;
- other services;
- other occupations not classified above.

Fig. S.8 uses this classification to show how the labour forces of France and Tanzania differ with regard to the type of work done. Classification can be further simplified by grouping jobs and industries into four large and broad categories of economic activity, known as sectors:

■ *The Primary Activities Sector* – this covers the first and second groups listed above. Agriculture is the main single activity in primary industry. The term *extractive industry* is often used to describe activities in this sector because they are concerned with the extraction of material from land or sea.

■ *The Secondary Activities Sector* – manufacturing which uses the products of primary industry and processes them into finished goods is secondary industry. The third and fourth groups listed above, which include building and construction work, fall into this sector.

■ *The Tertiary Activities Sector* – the fifth, seventh and eighth groups listed above are concerned with the provision of services rather than goods. The production is of intangible and invisible items that cannot be touched, felt or readily seen, like the outputs of a banker, train driver and teacher.

■ *The Quaternary Activities Sector* – this last category is a relatively new addition to the occupational classification by sector. Research work, higher education (university lecturers), the so-called professions (doctors, lawyers, etc.) and other services concerned with providing information and expertise are covered. Such occupations may barely exist in some countries (Fig. S.9)

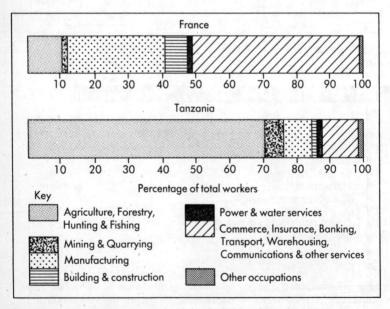

Fig. S.8 A comparison between the type of work done by the labour forces of France and Tanzania

Country	Primary	Secondary	Tertiary/ Quaternary	GNP per head ($US 1986)
India	72	13	15	260
France	12	36	52	9 760
Greece	36	29	35	3 770
Japan	12	39	49	10 630
Mexico	40	24	36	2 040
Netherlands	7	33	60	9 520
New Zealand	12	33	55	7 730
Sweden	6	38	56	11 860
Tanzania	75	11	14	210
Uganda	85	5	10	230

Fig. S.9 The percentage of the workforce employed in the four sectors of industry and the origin of GNP per head

The proportion of workers employed in each of the various sectors can be presented diagrammatically by either bar chart (Fig. S.8), pie chart (Fig. S.10) or triangular graph (Fig. S.11). Each diagram shows that as a country develops economically, the proportion of its labour force employed in the primary sector declines while the secondary sector grows in importance; continued economic development sees the eventual decline of secondary industry and the rise of the tertiary and quaternary sectors.

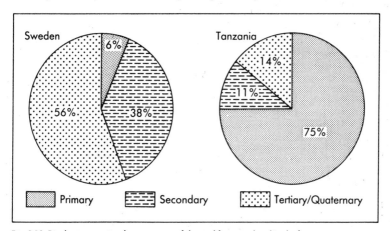

Fig. S.10 Pie chart comparing the percentage of the workforce employed in the four sectors of industry in Sweden and in Tanzania

The transition from secondary to service industries in the UK between 1950 and 1985 has been a major cause of unemployment. Fig. S.12 shows a model of a country's changing employment structure as it develops economically. The structure of employment also varies within a country.

◄ Tertiary producer ►

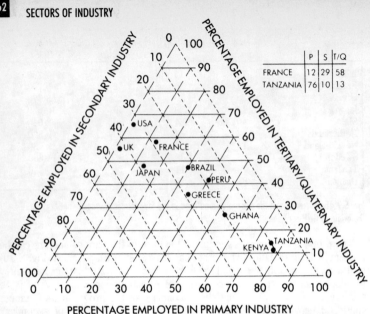

	P	S	T/Q
FRANCE	12	29	58
TANZANIA	76	10	13

Fig. S.11 Triangular graph to show the employment structure of selected countries

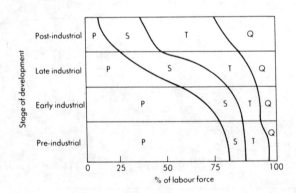

P = Primary industry
S = Secondary industry
T = Tertiary industry
Q = Quaternary industry

Fig. S.12 Stages in the economic development of a country and changes in its employment structure

SHANTY TOWNS

A shanty town is an illegal squatter settlement built of tents and shacks made out of scrap material on unoccupied land on the edge of or within the city. They develop spontaneously and grow very quickly; the number of migrants from the countryside is so large that the city authorities cannot house them. They arrive penniless but hope 'to make it' in the city.

Shanty towns are features of many large cities, especially in the developing world. While they are usually to be found on unused land on the edge of the city, there are examples on unused land within the city. For example, Bombay, India has had its shanties spring up on vacant land in the **central business district**, and street dwellings are common in many Indian cities.

Many shanty towns lack all public facilities (e.g., water supply, drains, etc.) at the beginning of their life, but in time they often develop facilities (e.g., stand pipes for water, an electricity line, etc.). Homes may be improved and the camp may become a fully fledged district or suburb of the city. Half of Mexico City's 14 million people live in shanty towns, either new or more permanent ones. Many of the developing world's **million cities** have between a quarter and a third of their population living in such areas. These figures do not include people living legally in the city's slums.

All cities in both the developed and developing world, including London, have slum areas and city poverty.

Shanty towns, with their illegal squatters, have different local names around the developing world: for example, *favela* in Brazil; *bustee* in Calcutta; *barriada* in Peru; *gecekundu* in Turkey; *barong-barongs* in the Philippines; *callampas* in Chile.

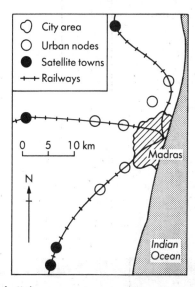

Fig. S.13 A master plan for Madras

Government policies to deal with the problems caused by the development of shanty towns have ranged from police action and the knocking down of the shanties to efforts to improve them by supplying water and power services, making legal the land holding and supporting the establishment of schools, clinics, etc. Many shanty town dwellers show co-operation and respect for property and self-help. The shanty town problem may also be eased by reducing the migration to the cities in the first place; schemes to reduce rural poverty may help in this respect.

Madras, India's fourth largest city, has tried to overcome its squatter problem by planning, building new, far better-chosen sites for migrants, properly laid out, with transport and essential services provided. This is the so-called master plan for Madras (Fig. S.13), first published in 1975. The main features were a series of urban nodes and satellite towns designed to relieve congestion and pressure in the city proper.

There were to be six urban nodes (an urban node is simply a new, planned concentration of urban growth), all close to the city and connected to it by public transport, and each planned to contain a population of between 200,000 and 300,000. Beyond the urban nodes, about 20 kilometres from the edge of the city, four new satellite towns were to be built, each one of which would be self-sufficient in terms of employment and facilities, commerce and housing.

SHIFTING CULTIVATION

This is a farming practice common in some tropical areas, especially rainforest in Africa and South America. New farmland is brought into use by clearing the trees using slash-and-burn techniques. The newly cleared field is then cultivated with, for example, groundnuts. Soil exhaustion tends to occur relatively quickly on deforested land in a wet climate. When yields fall, the land is left fallow (uncultivated), during which time it is likely to become vegetated by bush (young trees, bushes and undergrowth). Shifting cultivation is also known as *bush fallowing* for this reason, especially when the villagers have merely left the soil to recover its fertility and plan to reuse the field again in the future. Bush fallowing depends entirely on judging accurately the length of the soil-nutrient cycle for its success, allowing the soil sufficient time to recover its fertility before recultivation begins. Bush fallowing can break down when the length of the fallow period is reduced, perhaps because of the pressure of increased population and food demand.

Shifting cultivation involves moving cultivation to a newly cleared field from an abandoned field, which may or may not be recultivated in the future. Abandoning and never recultivating fields is a destructive practice, increasing deforestation.

SINUOSITY

◀ Meanders ▶

The site of a settlement, a factory or any geographical feature is the actual piece of ground on which it stands. This is its absolute location rather than its relative location (its position in relation to other features), which is known as situation. Site and situation are the two kinds of location recognised by geographers.

Many large cities began as a market and meeting place by a ford (a shallow point of a river which could be crossed on foot) where bridges were later built. All settlements, however large now, obviously must have had an original building site. They can be classified according to this original site. Would-be settlers could be expected to choose sites which offered a water supply, a fuel supply, a supply of building materials, farmland for grazing and growing crops, good trading possibilities (e.g., where routes naturally met) and were easy to defend against intruders.

Five different types of settlement site are shown in Fig. S.14. It is not difficult to see that water supply, meeting points of routeways and defensibility were important considerations.

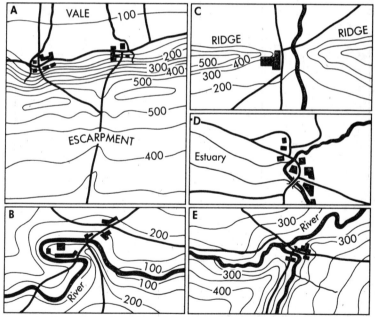

A   Spring-line settlement – at the point where springs are found
B   Defensive site – an easily defended place, usually a hill
C   Gap site – a place where it is easy to pass between two ridges
D   Lowest bridging point – the place nearest the sea where a river can be bridged
E   Confluence site – where 2 or more rivers join

Fig. S.14 Five different types of settlement

SOIL EROSION

This is the removal of the soil by erosional agents, especially water and wind. Soil erosion is a consequence of **mass movement** and the processes responsible for soil erosion are mass-movement processes (e.g., soil creep). However, as soil erosion is principally a farming problem, it must be remembered that major soil erosion is often connected with poor agricultural practices; for example, the overgrazing of an area by farm animals, causing the destruction of the vegetation cover and a loss of protection and binding for the soil; the clearing of forest for farmland, which frequently has a similar effect; the wrong ploughing of sloping fields.

Fig. S.15 suggests why terracing (cutting steps into a hillside with a small wall or bank to retain the soil and water on the farmed step), contour ploughing (ploughing around a slope, parallel to the contours, rather than up and down it) and strip cropping (the division of a field into strips so that the crops in each can be rotated, which means that as little of the field as possible is uncropped and unprotected from erosion at any time, and the demands on the soil are lessened, so reducing the risk of erosion through low soil quality) are commonly used methods of preventing soil erosion. Contour ploughing is the most effective method of soil conservation on slopes in temperate climates.

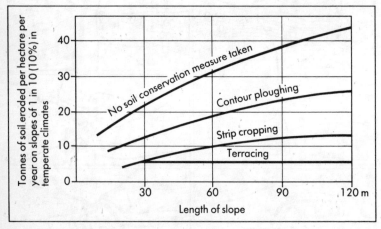

Fig. S.15 The advantages of terracing to combat soil erosion

Weather elements, mainly wind and rain, keep soil constantly on the move, and at times strong wind can quickly remove good topsoil, blowing clouds of dust far afield. The natural grasslands of the western USA became known as the Dust Bowl in the 1930s after strong winds and drought were responsible for the erosion of dry, overploughed soil. These dust storms left the area an agricultural desert and led to large-scale migration of the farming population. The state of Oklahoma was particularly affected by such soil erosion, caused by a combination of human misuse of land and the natural results of physical geography.

SPHERE OF INFLUENCE

Large settlements (towns and cities) tend to exert an influence upon their surrounding areas and in turn are influenced by them. This surrounding area which the town/city serves and which in turn supports the town/city is said to be its sphere of influence, urban field or hinterland. The concept of a sphere of influence results from the fact that the number and order of functions available depends on the size and importance of a settlement. Only in larger settlements are middle- and high-order functions provided, that is, they have a higher threshold population and people are willing to travel for goods and services; some items have a range of many miles.

Fig. S.16 which shows the population and a number of selected services available in ten settlements in a region of Britain, illustrates these ideas.

Settlement	Population	Services/functions			
		Grocery stores	Banks	Woolworth's	Marks and Spencer
A	56 000	36	25	1	1
B	35 000	25	11	1	
C	19 000	19	6	1	
D	12 000	14	5		
E	12 000	10	5		
F	9 000	7	2		
G	7 000	6	2		
H	6 000	7	1		
I	3 500	4	1		
J	2 600	2			

Fig. S.16

It is possible to define the sphere of influence of a town/city in two ways. First by extensive interviewing of customers and certain major shops and services in a large settlement. Bus timetables, delivery areas of department stores, etc. provide valuable information. Desire lines can be drawn and from them it may be possible to deduce a sphere of influence. Second, it can be calculated theoretically using a formula which gives you the so-called *breakpoint of attraction* between two settlements. Breakpoint refers to the sphere of influence boundary between two settlements. It is possible to establish a theoretical sphere of influence for a town/city using this formula, and then perhaps to test how accurate it really is by doing some interview fieldwork. Fig. S.17 shows the service area of three functions provided by Middlesbrough: the town's sphere of influence may be determined from such information.

Spheres of influence often overlap, as Fig. S.18 indicates. Where towns ranging in size are near to each other, the sphere of influence of smaller settlements may lie wholly or partly within that of the larger settlement. Spheres of influence may change their size and shape as a result of competition from surrounding towns and changes in transport facilities.

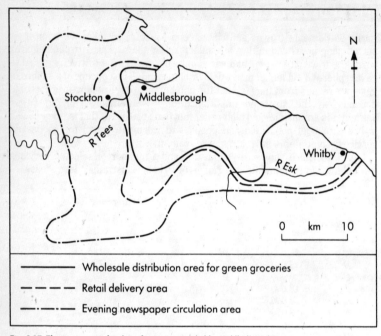

Fig. S.17 The service area for three functions provided by Middlesbrough

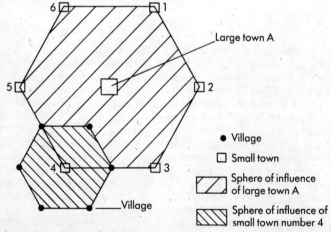

Fig. S.18 Overlapping spheres of influence

The concept of a sphere of influence applies to individual shops, out-of-town shopping centres, international airports, etc. They all draw customers from a wider area, from areas of varying extent.

STACK

A stack is an isolated pillar of rock in the sea close to cliffs. It represents a short stage in the recession (erosion backwards) of a cliffed coastline.

In Fig. S.19 the Old Harry Rocks are examples of stacks. They were previously part of the land and later were probably the outer wall of an arch, now collapsed. Arches are generally thought to have developed from sea caves (Fig. S.20), formed at large joints or weaknesses in the rocks during the general undercutting, collapse and recession of the cliffs.

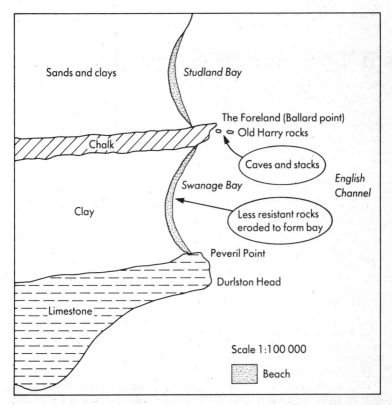

Fig. S.19 The Dorset coast showing Old Harry Rocks

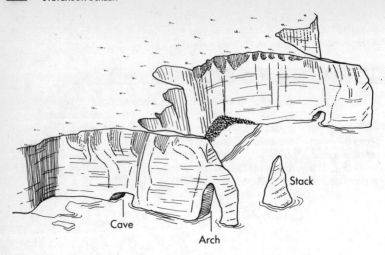

Fig. S.20 The development of a stack from an arch and a cave

STEVENSON SCREEN

This is a thermometer screen built to house thermometers measuring certain standard outdoor temperatures. It is a white wooden box with louvred sides to allow air to flow through it and to minimise heat absorption by the box itself. The thermometers used are likely to be a minimum thermometer (Fig. S.21) and a hygrometer (Fig. S.22). It also has a double roof as insulation against direct sunlight, and stands in the open 1.2 metres above ground level.

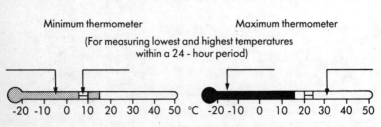

Fig. S.21 Minimum and maximum thermometers

Standard shade temperatures are measured in a Stevenson Screen (shade temperatures indicating the temperature of the air are standard throughout the world).

The positioning of weather-recording instruments to obtain accurate readings which will be used in comparisons with readings taken elsewhere is very important. A possible arrangement of the instrument area of a weather station is given in Fig. S.23.

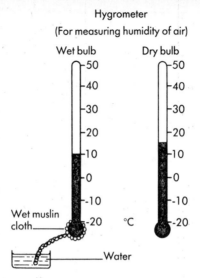

Fig. S.22 A hygrometer

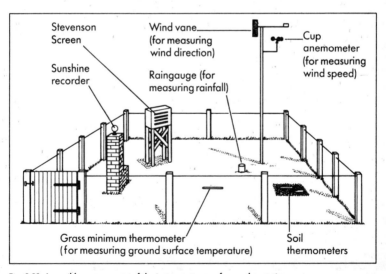

Fig. S.23 A possible arrangement of the instrument area of a weather station

Fig. S.24 shows maximum temperatures recorded in the shade and on the ground surface in various tropical desert regions. These are some of the highest temperatures ever recorded in the world.

Shade temperatures		Ground surface temperatures	
Location	Extreme Maximum (°C)	Location	Mean Maximum (°C)
Azizia (Libya)	58	Red Sea Hills (Egypt)	82
Death Valley (USA)	57	Insalah (Libya)	78
Tindouf (Algeria)	57	Kalahari (Namibia)	72
Insalah (Libya)	54	Tucson (USA)	71
William Creek (Australia)	48	Death Valley (USA)	70

Fig. S.24 Maximum temperatures recorded in tropical desert regions

STREAM VELOCITY

The speed or velocity at which the water in a stream or river flows can be measured using either simple devices, such as an orange or table-tennis ball and stop watch, or more sophisticated instruments, such as a flowmeter. The velocity is affected by the gradient of the bed of the channel; streams may be fast-flowing because of their steeply sloping beds. Average velocity often remains steady or increases downstream because of the declining roughness of the bed and banks of the channel; friction is reduced. Velocities generally increase during flood, when discharge of the stream or river is higher and it is at bankful level. They also vary across the channel (Fig. S.25).

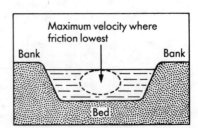

Fig. S.25 Stream velocity varies across a channel

SUBSISTENCE FARMING

For a large proportion of the population of **developing countries** farming is the only means of livelihood, despite the recent drift of people to the towns. Low production for the large number of farmers and from each hectare leads to food shortage. Subsistence farmers living in poverty make up much of the large rural population.

The low production and poverty among farmers which exists in much of the developing world is the result of a vicious circle (Fig. S.26), and breaking this circle of underdevelopment has proved difficult. Some of the attempts that have been and are being made are part of the **green revolution**.

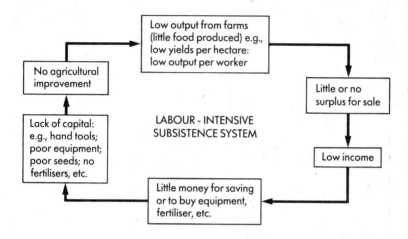

Fig. S.26 Low output farms in developing countries

The villages of the Ganges Delta depend upon subsistence rice farming. Rice is the staple food of most of South-East Asia. The paddy (unhusked rice) is grown in small plots in widely scattered fields covered by water during the growing season. It is a type of farming very well adapted to local conditions and closely related to climate and population (Fig. S.27):

- the growing season is timed to benefit from the high rainfall of the monsoon. Level relief, perhaps achieved by cutting terraces into sloping land, is important for flooding the fields.
- the farming is very labour-intensive in this area of high population densities. The land is intensively farmed, using a large labour force. Productivity levels per worker are low and largely subsistent. Capital inputs are generally small.

The system, though subsistent, does generally meet the large demand for food. By using fertilisers, higher-yielding varieties or buying the land they farm, more progressive farmers have been able to raise their output and become commercial farmers. Where IR8 rice has been grown, higher yield and two crops a year (multiple cropping) have been achieved.

◀ Commercial farming, Food supply ▶

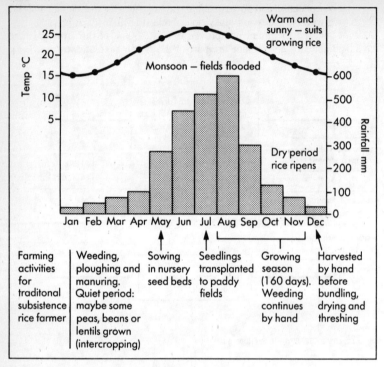

Fig. S.27 The climate of the Ganges Delta, north-east India

SUPERSTORE

In the USA huge shopping schemes, which include hypermarkets, have been built on the outskirts of many towns and cities, surrounded by facilities such as cinemas, restaurants, swimming pools and playgrounds. Brent Cross in north London and the Metro Centre in Newcastle are examples of the change towards the American locational pattern of out-of-town shopping. Out-of-town superstores owned by a few leading retailers (e.g., Asda, Tesco, Sainsbury's) have been replacing small independent shops (Fig. S.28). It is said that one new supermarket replaces between ten and fifteen small shops. Has bigger been better in retailing?

Some of the effects of the superstore revolution in Britain are:

- some people have further to travel to shop – a problem for the old and infirm, and for those without their own transport or living where public transport is inconvenient or unreliable;
- congestion and pollution in the suburbs due to the increased use of cars for shopping;
- loss of large areas of countryside for purpose-built superstores and their car parks;

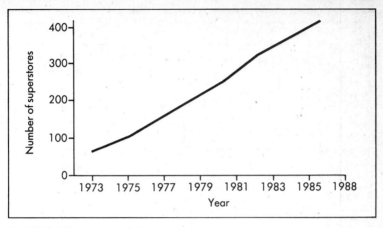

Fig. S.28 The UK superstore revolution

- loss of shops in villages and suburbs;
- 'one-stop' shopping (with a wide range of goods under one roof); using the car and free on-site parking makes shopping convenient and easy;
- people have to shop less often but have to buy their own storage facilities (e.g., freezers).
- less expensive prices are charged because buying and selling can be in bulk;
- restricted choice of brands for shoppers.

The development of out-of-town shopping centres is threatening to kill town-centre trade in many British towns/cities. There is a growing conflict between established town centre shopping and new out-of-town shopping centres. Local authority Planning Departments, faced with this conflict, consider the following points when deciding whether to grant planning permission for new superstores:

- will it harm the future of shops in established shopping centres?
- will it be readily served by public transport?
- will it cause traffic congestion?
- will it harm the amenities of the surrounding area?

SYSTEMS (FARMING SYSTEMS)

Farms can be studied as food-producing systems. Food is an output from the farming system, produced when inputs to the system (e.g., seed, machinery, labour combine with the processes of farming e.g., ploughing, feeding. Farm inputs, processes and outputs can be drawn as a systems diagram (Fig. S.29). Each farm works as an input-process-output system. A change in one of these parts of the system affects other parts (e.g., output should rise if the farmer increases input). Farmers in developing countries trying to increase food production have to increase the input into their farming system e.g., more

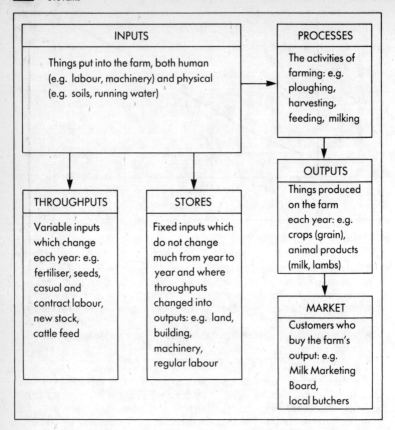

Fig. S.29 Farming as a system

land, more fertilisers. In a system input influences output; you get out in food only what you put in in input! A system is integrated and the relationships or links between all parts are shown on a systems diagram by arrows.

A farm is a business and has to make money. From the sale of the farm's output, the farmer receives income, some of which must go to pay for the cost of inputs e.g., rent, wages, fertiliser bills. Any remaining income is profit and the farmer must decide how much of any profit is to be reinvested and how much can be taken for personal spending. This decision-making point and the way money as an output from the system can be fed back to become an input are shown.

Farming systems differ from place to place and from time to time. Fig. S.30 shows the differences between a mixed commercial farm in Britain and a subsistence farm in Sri Lanka. 200 years ago some farms in Britain would have operated in the same way as the Sri Lankan model.

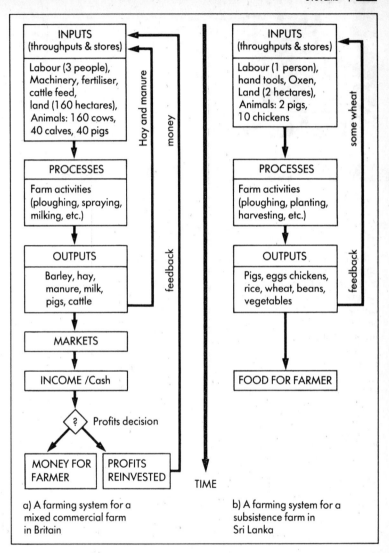

Fig. S.30 Contrasting farming systems

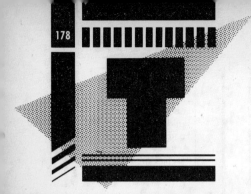

TECTONICS

◀ Plate tectonics ▶

TEMPERATURE INVERSION

An inversion is the exact opposite of the normal **lapse rate** in the lower atmosphere, that is, the lapse rate is inverted. There is an increase in temperature from the ground layer upwards. It is commonly experienced in hollows and valleys, especially in winter on calm, clear nights. A winter **anticyclone** will produce these clear conditions and rapid cooling through the **radiation** of heat from the Earth's surface. Cold air will sink under the influence of gravity into hollows and valleys, leading to the formation of cold, motionless air and dense fog (a frost-hollow). Warmer air will lie above this cold layer.

Cities, with their industry and large numbers of motor cars, built in hollows, are particularly prone to inversions and fog (Fig. T.1). Pollution from industry and car exhausts encourages the formation of fog (e.g., in Los Angeles).

In farming valleys, especially those growing crops sensitive to frost such as fruit, farmers often avoid using the valley-bottom land and ensure that there are no obstacles like solid walls on the valley side behind which cold air could be trapped.

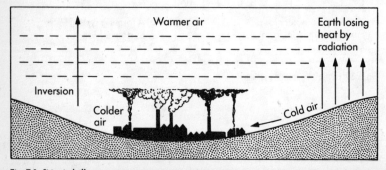

Fig. T.1 Cities in hollows are prone to temperature inversion

TERTIARY PRODUCER

A very large proportion of the working population of **developed countries** is no longer employed in agriculture or manufacturing but in services (tertiary activities).

More than half of London's jobs are in the service sector (e.g., wholesale and retail distribution, government and administration, etc.) Service sector jobs can be split into quaternary activities (top decision-making jobs like research workers, doctors, lawyers, senior managers) and tertiary activities (all the other service jobs). Employment in shops, offices and other establishments providing services (e.g., hotels) has grown rapidly in recent years in 'developed' countries as:

- the needs and demands of people have become more complex. The supply and range of services has increased.
- working hours have fallen and the amount of **leisure** time has increased. The 'leisure age' and a more leisure-orientated life has emerged.
- economic growth has raised income levels per head so that people can afford to be more pleasure-seeking.
- manufacturing, particularly heavy manufacturing (e.g., textiles, mining, etc.) has declined.

In **developed countries** the service sector tends to be smaller but it is there (e.g., government and business offices, street traders, etc.). Most services tend to develop later in a country's economic development, once its basic needs (e.g., food, household goods, etc.) have been met.

Service activities are strongly attracted to large urban centres, being located near demand, that is, they are customer-oriented. City centres consist of government and commercial offices, shops, entertainment, hotels and public/social services like libraries. Office work is a growing industry (Fig. T.2), employing around a third of the British workforce. Clustering at city

Country	Office jobs as % of total number of jobs	
	1960	1980
France	20.2	31.7
New Zealand	27.9	32.2
Sweden	23.5	40.9
UK	24.0	34.1
USA	31.7	41.1

Fig. T.2 Office jobs in five developed countries

centre locations is common, especially among commercial offices (e.g., insurance companies, solicitors, etc.) because:

- they need strong links with other offices and associated businesses (e.g., estate agents, solicitors, banks and building societies, all concerned with buying and selling houses, find it convenient to be close together so that

face-to-face contact is possible). Modern telecommunications (e.g., telephone calls, telex machines, computer terminals, etc.) have reduced the necessity for offices to cluster around other offices.
- they are the most accessible sites for both staff and customers.
- it is the traditional office area which carries prestige, is very visible to the public, has access to business contacts and other services for the staff, and has office premises available.

The skylines of cities show the high-rise office towerblocks at the centre, built upwards because of the competition for land.

◀ Sectors of industry ▶

THRESHOLD POPULATION

A minimum number of people must live in a settlement and its surrounding area before a particular service/function will be provided. The minimum number of people required to support a particular service/function is known as the threshold population value.

The table below gives the rough thresholds for a variety of low-, middle- and high-order functions.

Shop or service	Numbers of people living in the settlement and surrounding area	
General store	200	Low order
Primary school	250	Shops and services found in all towns and
Butcher	350	cities and most large villages. These
Newsagent	750	services are required by most people
Greengrocer	2,500	every week. Everyday goods and services
Post office	2,500	with a low threshold population.
Public house	3,500	
Doctor's surgery	3,500	
Branch library	12,000	Middle order
Bank	15,000	Shops and services found only in towns
Secondary school	17,000	and cities. Goods and services used and
Swimming pool	50,000	bought, say, two or three times a month.
Cinema	50,000	
Chain store (e.g., Boots)	50,000	
Museum	70,000	
Art gallery	200,000	High order
General hospital	200,000	Shops and services found only in major
Concert hall	300,000	towns and having a high threshold
Polytechnic/University	300,000	population.
Department store	350,000	

TILL

◀ Boulder clay ▶

TRAFFIC CONGESTION

Urban road traffic congestion is perhaps the biggest issue and problem in the geography of transport. Figs. T.3a) and T.3b) highlight the problem.

Move to 'bury' London's traffic crisis

Traffic-choked city on the road to nowhere

Figs. T.3a) and b) Newspaper headlines bemoaning traffic problems

Fig. T.4 shows changes in the volume of traffic during a weekday in a large city such as Manchester or London. The two peaks in the amount of traffic, numbered 1 and 2, result largely from journeys to and from work: the so-called 'rush hours'.

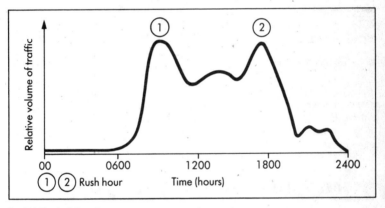

Fig. T.4 The 'rush hours'

Various transport improvements have been introduced into urban areas to help to solve this problem and the resulting concerns to people (e.g., delays to journeys, road traffic accidents, etc.). These include road-widening schemes, the building of inner relief roads and outer ring roads (urban motorways through the built-up area and around the suburbs or edge of the town/city), pedestrianising town centres so that they become traffic-free, turning town/city centre roads into one-way systems, developing tidal traffic flows along major roads, developing park-and-ride schemes (large, free suburban car parks with free bus services to and from the city centre) and the development of rapid transit systems (e.g., the London Docklands light railway. Sheffield's proposed supertram and the West Midland Metro, Fig. T.5, due to open in 1993 and join Birmingham and Wolverhampton by tram-like vehicles).

Fig. T.5 The West Midland metro

Vancouver, Canada, and San Francisco, USA, have working rapid transit systems known as Vancouver Rapid Transit and the Bay Area Rapid Transit system (BART for short) respectively. Both are systems of light passenger rail vehicles travelling on a track at ground level, in underground tunnels or above the ground. The systems can carry more passengers than other forms of urban transport (e.g., bus) because travel is far quicker.

TRANSNATIONAL COMPANIES

Transnational or multi-national companies are large international firms operating across national boundaries, often in dozens of countries, and exerting enormous influence over our lives. The people in charge may have more influence on the shape of society than many of our elected politicians. Fig. T.6 shows the fifteen largest of these companies, listed in rank order of their sales turnover in US dollars. These fifteen companies, plus a further thirty-two, and fifty-three countries make up the 100 most financially powerful organisations in the world.

Transnational companies have grown particularly quickly since the 1960s. There are now more companies than countries with incomes greater than the GNP of Ireland. In 1985 the sales turnover of the Royal Dutch/Shell Group of Companies was £73,000 million, and the GNPs of Argentina, Norway and Bangladesh were £67,000 million, £57,000 million and £13,000 million respectively. Fig. T.7 illustrates this point. The largest transitionals have turnovers greater than the combined GNPs of large groups of African countries.

Turnover ranking (in US $)	Company	Headquarters	Main Industries
1	Exxon (Esso)	New York	oil, chemicals
2	Royal Dutch/Shell Group	London/The Hague	oil, chemicals
3	General Motors	Detroit	cars, trucks
4	Ford Motors	Dearborn, Michigan	cars, trucks
5	Texaco	New York	oil
6	Mobil Oil	New York	oil
7	British Petroleum	London	oil, chemicals
8	Standard Oil of California	San Francisco	oil, chemicals
9	National Iranian Oil	Tehran	oil
10	Gulf Oil	Pittsburgh	oil, coal
11	Unilever	London	food, detergents
12	General Electric	Fairfield, Connecticut	electrical products
13	International Business Machines (IBM)	Armonk, New York	computers
14	International Tel. & Tel.	New York	telecommunications
15	Chrysler	Highland Park, Michigan	cars, trucks

Fig T.6 The fifteen largest companies in the world (1983)

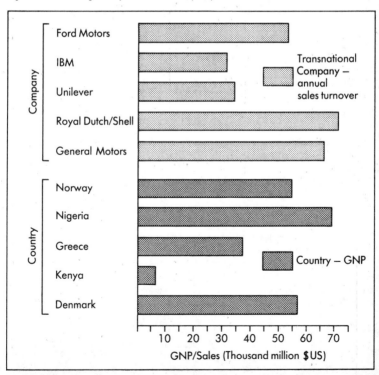

Fig. T.7 The total annual sales turnover of five transnational companies and the GNPs of five countries in 1985

Unilever PLC (UK) and Unilever NV (Netherlands) are parts of a transnational corporation composed of 8,000 firms, many multi-plant and multi-industry, making 1,200 different products and operating in seventy-five countries in all five continents. Products sold in Britain include Wall's Ice Cream, Birds Eye frozen foods, Lux, Lifebuoy and Pears soaps, Vesta foods, Stork margarine, Lipton's tea, Crisp N'Dry cooking oil, Signal toothpaste and Batchelor's Cup-a-Soup.

Unilever have firms throught the 'developing' world. In colonial times they started a large trading company in West Africa buying groundnut and palm oil for use in soap- and margarine-making for sale in Europe. Their operations in West Africa are now concerned with the manufacture of products like washing powder for local sale.

Foreign companies have an important influence upon the organisation of both manufacturing and agriculture in developing countries. This can have positive and negative effects. Fig. T.8 shows the main advantages and disadvantages of the build-up of foreign companies in 'developing' countries. It is clear that the factories, farms and jobs of a transnational company in a country will be part of a larger organisation and so may depend on processes and workers elsewhere, and will depend on decisions made elsewhere. The transnationals play a major part in 'developing' world agriculture. In many

Advantages of transnational companies	Disadvantages of transnational companies
provide money (capital and foreign exchange) for development	make profits in 'developing' countries, often sending more of them back home than they invest locally
provide jobs for local people	can undercut local prices and drive local firms out of business, so causing some job losses
introduce new technology	hire mostly unskilled local people, with many skilled and management jobs being held by foreigners
produce useful products for the local market which might otherwise have to be imported (e.g. oil, cars)	may produce goods not appropriate to 'developing' countries, but being foreign carry status, especially with rich (e.g., Nestle's powdered baby milk)
often pay higher wages than local firms	attracted by cheap, controllable labour, especially female, and pay less than to workers doing same job in 'developed' countries
are a cause of change, and progress (economic growth)	often borrow local capital rather than import it and so deprive local industry of finance
	technology is often imported, with Research and Development work staying in the 'developed' countries

Fig. T.8 The advantages and disadvantages of transnational companies for developing countries former colonial, now 'developing' countries plantation commodities (e.g., tea, coffee) grown for export to **developed countries** dominate agriculture (rather than staple foods for local consumption) and the whole economy. For instance, in Sri Lanka such products, especially tea, take up twice the land area used for growing local food crops and account for 76 per cent of the country's foreign earnings. Transnationals such as:

- Unilever, Brooke-Bond Liebig, sell 85 per cent of world tea exports;
- Nestlé, General Foods, sell 85 per cent of world coffee exports;
- Geest, Del Monte, sell 70 per cent of world banana exports;
- Tate and Lyle sell 60 per cent of world sugar exports.

This situation means that decisions about what is grown and about prices are made outside the developing countries, very much influenced by transnationals. Decisions made at the company's headquarters can vitally affect the countries in which it operates; decisions made in the interests of the company may be against the interests of these countries. General Motors, with subsidiaries around the world like Vauxhall and Opel, are able to switch production from one country to another and so affect the livelihoods of working people. In an effort to curb the worst effects of this, the Brandt Report of 1980 suggested that the governments of both 'North' and 'South' developed a 'code of conduct' to control the actions of these massive companies.

TRANSPORT NETWORK

A transport network is a pattern of roads, railways, canals, etc. which connect places. Networks consist of nodes (towns, factories, etc.) and links or edges (roads, railways, telephone communications, etc.) which join up the nodes to form a network. Networks are built for various reasons. For example, they enable people to visit friends and business people, and to buy things from other countries that cannot be home-grown (e.g., tropical fruits).

Fig. T.9 shows the road network of the Isle of Wight.

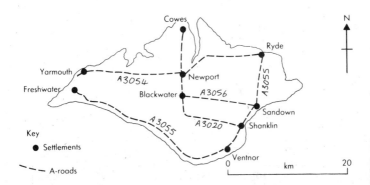

Fig. T.9 The road network of the Isle of Wight

Transport networks are often shown as topological maps, that is, maps drawn to show only certain important relationships. Locations are represented by dots and the links between them by straight lines; distances, scale and directions may be inaccurate (Fig. T.10).

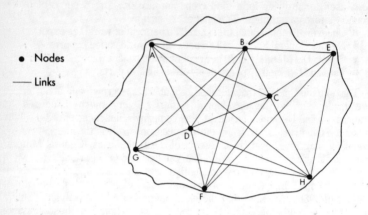

Fig. T.10 Topological transport network map

TRANSPORT REVOLUTION

One of the greatest changes in people's lives, particularly in the developed world over the last 100 years, has been the possibility of much greater mobility. The vast majority of the population of Britain 100 years ago were born, married, lived all their lives and died within the same few square miles; they had little or no contact with and knowledge of the world beyond their

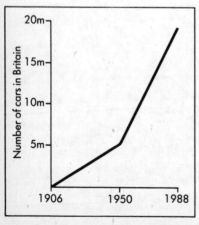

Fig. T.11 The number of cars in Britain (1988)

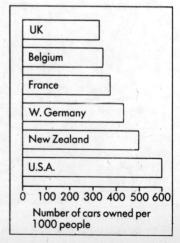

immediate area! The general increase in mobility and changes in transport, especially over the past thirty years, have been so great that they can be described as a revolution. For instance, the number of cars in Britain has increased about ten times over the past forty years (Fig. T.11). However, car ownership in Britain is not high within the developed world (Fig. T.12).

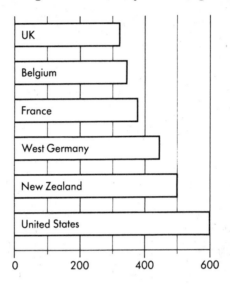

Fig. T.12 National car ownership per 1,000 (1988)

The principal means of travel within Britain between 1975 and 1985 were:

	Billion kms of travel	
	1975	1985
Road (car and taxi)	294	426
Road (bus and coach)	55	42
Rail	35	36
Air	2	4

Air travel abroad by British people also shows a dramatic increase. The number of passengers using Heathrow, Gatwick, Stansted, Glasgow, Edinburgh, Prestwick and Aberdeen airports rose from 43 millions in 1983 to 65 millions in 1988.

Developments in transport and communication often allow other changes to take place, including the economic development of an area. Without transport improvements, development cannot occur. An efficient transport network is the basis of the highly industrialised economies of the USA, Japan, etc. The right distribution of materials, labour, ideas and products is essential.

Fig. T.13, for example, shows there to be a positive correlation between the number of vehicles in the countries of Latin America and their Gross National Products (GNPs). The levels of transport and economic development are related.

◀ Motorways ▶

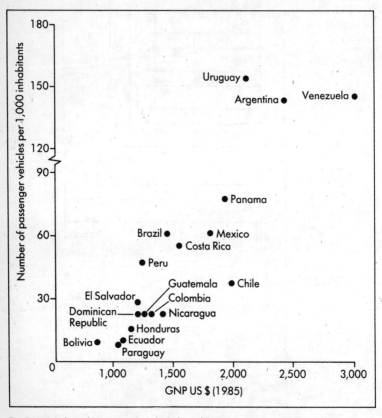

Fig. T.13 Correlation between number of vehicles and GNP in Latin America

TRIANGULAR GRAPH

The great advantage of this type of graph is that it enables you to plot three sets of data on one diagram. A carefully drawn triangle-shaped framework has to be available first, though!

Triangular graphs are commonly used in GCSE geography to show the percentage of workers in each of the **sectors of industry** – primary, secondary and tertiary/quaternary-in a country.

Plotting the data and reading plotted data off a triangular graph (Fig. S.11) can be a problem. The technique is shown in the smaller graph, Fig. T.14.

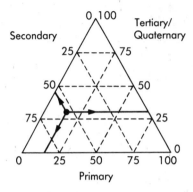

Fig. T.14 Simplified triangular graph showing percentage of workers in each of the sectors of industry

TUNDRA

◄ Boulder clay ►

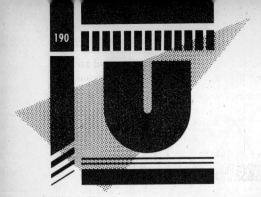

URBAN CLIMATES

Studies show that urban areas receive 15 per cent less sunshine, 10 per cent more **precipitation** (rain, hail and snow) and have lower visibility than rural areas. Fog is 30 per cent more frequent in summer and 100 per cent more frequent in winter, and cloudy days are 10 per cent more frequent over the year as a whole. However, urban areas are generally between 2° and 6°C warmer and wind speeds are generally lower. Cities have climates that differ from those of the surrounding country areas. They tend to experience higher air temperatures (the **heat island** effect), lower wind speeds because of the greater friction and drag which buildings place on the wind, and have more air pollution, largely because of industrial emissions and traffic exhausts. This is a major factor in the lower visibility and greater incidence of cloud and fog in cities.

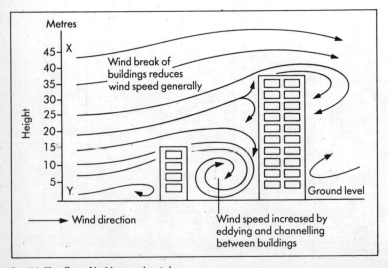

Fig. U.1 The effects of buildings on the wind

Fig. U.1 shows the effect of buildings in a city on the wind, and how its speeds are generally reduced but can be greater in places because of turbulence, eddying and channelling.

URBAN SPRAWL

Urban sprawl is the process involved in **urbanisation**. Towns and cities grow outwards spreading into the countryside. Sprawl can be a result of ribbon development along major roads, as shown in Fig. U.2. Outlying villages become suburbs of the town/city, as can be seen in Fig. U.3.

Urban sprawl through suburbanisation can proceed to such an extent that towns and cities merge, producing a conurbation. It has been predicted that if urban sprawl continues at its present pace in south-east England, in the next century a massive, continuously built-up area will cover the region.

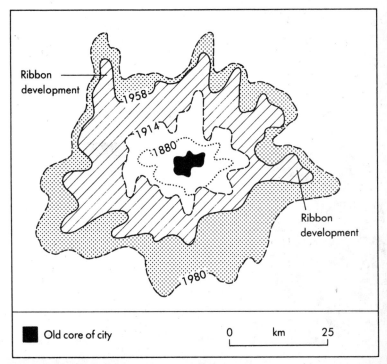

Fig. U.2 Ribbon development affecting city boundary, 1880–1980

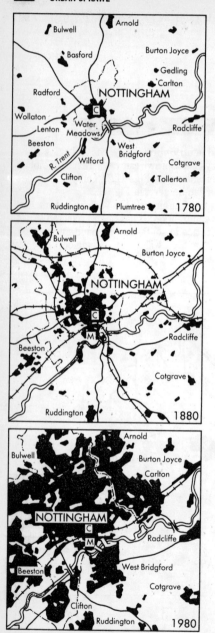

Fig. U.3 Urban sprawl and Nottingham, 1780–1980

Census information collected from households along a north–south, east–west profile across a town/city will show significant contrasts in the way people live and the environment in which they live (Fig. U.6).

Censuses are held every ten years in Britain. Every household has to provide information about itself. Later, data for each administrative area (ward) is available. Fig. U.4 shows data for wards in Chesterfield, Derbyshire.

Ward	Population change (%) 1971–1981	Household with no car (%)	Households with no inside WC (%)	Residents born outside UK (%)	Households owner-occupied (%)
Inkersall	+20.4	33.2	0	1.4	44.4
St Helens	−10.3	60.2	4.6	4.6	33.3
Walton	+52.3	18.5	0.9	2.8	90.9
West	+7.1	29.7	2.8	1.9	86.5
Barrow Hill & Hollingswood	−5.2	57.5	12.5	1.3	8.4
Holmebrook	+4.6	59.5	10.4	3.6	49.8
Markham	−34.2	62.8	0.2	0.2	3.6

Fig. U.4 Census data for Chesterfield wards

Contrasts can be seen in a variety of aspects of life, including:
- population change – old inner areas of towns/cities tend to have decreasing populations and newer, outer areas have population increase.
- housing tenure (ownership) – the percentage of owner-occupied houses tends to increase towards the outer edge of towns/cities.
- housing quality and household amenities – again, the general trend is improvement out towards the residential suburbs, especially on the western side of the town/city. Plumbing facilities (e.g., inside toilets, hot water supply), the cost of housing and the number of rooms per person (housing density) reflect this trend.
- population density – as Fig. U.5 indicates, this tends to fall as you move from the inner to the outer suburbs of the town/city.

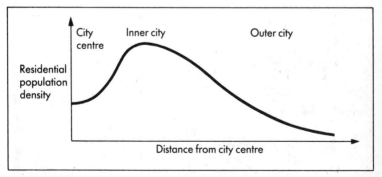

Fig. U.5 Population density

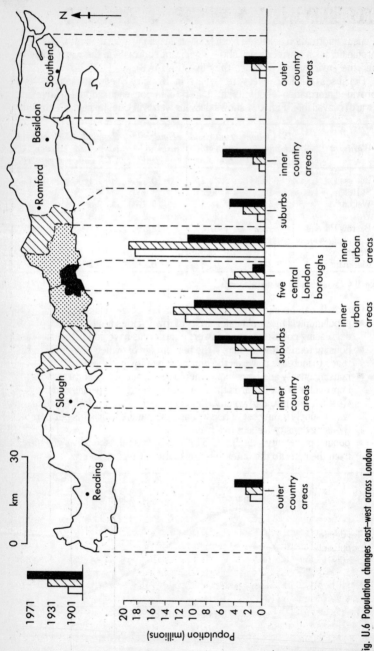

Fig. U.6 Population changes east–west across London

- open space – as Fig. U.7 indicates, the amount of open space (e.g., woodland, public parks, etc.) increases away from the city centre.

Contrasts in a range of other areas, such as type of housing (size, building materials, gardens, detached, semi-detached or terraced), socio-economic group of residents (their jobs), age of residents, car ownership, number of residents born outside the UK etc.

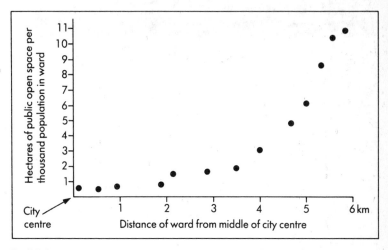

Fig. U.7 Open space

URBAN ZONES

Within the same town or city some areas are very different from others. Land is used in totally different ways.

A description of a journey outwards from the centre of large British cities such as Birmingham, Sheffield, Manchester and Bristol may take the following form. Travelling outwards along the low-lying land by the river, with the wind behind us, we passed through warehouses, heavy industry and derelict land. Next came streets of poor, crowded houses and council flats, and beyond them the less fashionable suburbs. Travelling outwards on the other side of the city, uphill and into the prevailing wind, we passed the city hall, the banks and lawyers, then the university, main hospital and medical school, the most famous secondary schools and Victorian mansions now converted into flats. Beyond them stood inter-war semi-detached houses, growing new suburbs, and finally commuter villages.

The pattern of land use everywhere is not as clear-cut as this, but urban land-use zones do exist in all towns/cities and they often conform to the west end/upwind/higher-income housing and east end/downwind/industrial suburbs pattern described (Fig. U.8).

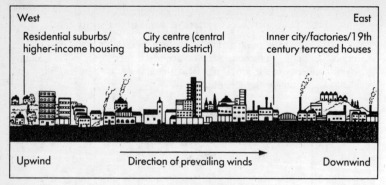

Fig. U.8 The skyline of a large city in the developed world

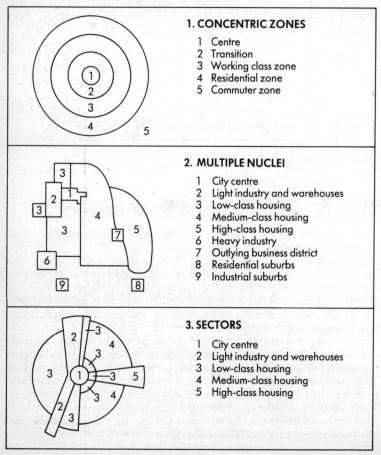

1. CONCENTRIC ZONES

1 Centre
2 Transition
3 Working class zone
4 Residential zone
5 Commuter zone

2. MULTIPLE NUCLEI

1 City centre
2 Light industry and warehouses
3 Low-class housing
4 Medium-class housing
5 High-class housing
6 Heavy industry
7 Outlying business district
8 Residential suburbs
9 Industrial suburbs

3. SECTORS

1 City centre
2 Light industry and warehouses
3 Low-class housing
4 Medium-class housing
5 High-class housing

Fig. U.9a) Urban models

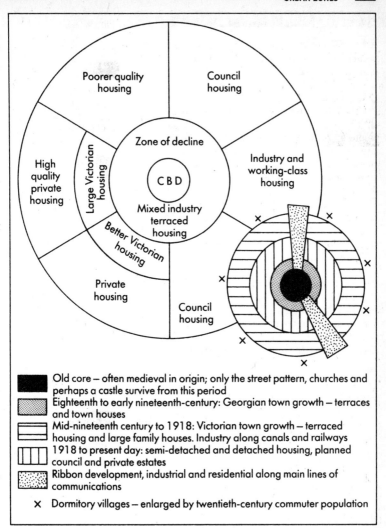

Fig. U.9b) Urban models

The various functions of a settlement tend not to be scattered throughout the area of the settlement, but clustered in certain areas. These clusters of similar land use are known as urban zones. There have been various attempts by geographers to discover any general pattern in the arrangement of urban zones. Four simplified urban models have been produced and towns/cities fit one or a combination of these models to varying extents (Fig. U.9). Note that the fourth model, the Integrated Model, is an attempt to represent 'typical' British towns/cities by combining rings and sectors.

URBANISATION

About 30 per cent of the world's population live in urban areas, that is, settlements with a population greater than 20,000 (towns and cities). The percentage is increasing. In Britain the percentage was roughly 25 in 1800; it is nearer 80 today. This increase in the number of people living in towns and cities is called urbanisation.

Urbanisation tends to accompany industrialisation. The industrialisation of Britain and the mechanisation of agriculture during the eighteenth and nineteenth centuries resulted in rapid growth in the size of settlements, largely through migration from the countryside (rural areas). Until recently, cities in the developed world have become increasingly bigger and more numerous. There is a recent trend for large cities to lose population. Between the 1971 and 1981 census London lost 18 per cent of its population, Manchester 17 per cent and Liverpool 16 per cent. This is not the trend in the developing world, where the rate of increase of the urban population has in many cases been phenomenal. For example, Sao Paulo, Brazil, grew approximately 150 per cent between 1970 and 1985.

Settlements are never stationary but, as living organisms, are always dynamically on the move. The process of urbanisation is always the same: migration into the town/city, with the result that suburbs grow, reaching out into rurban (the rural-urban fringe). The term **urban sprawl** is used to describe this process.

Four stages in the development of a settlement in the developed world are shown in Fig. U.10. Industrialisation and suburbanisation have been responsible for the growth in population (the urbanisation of the area).

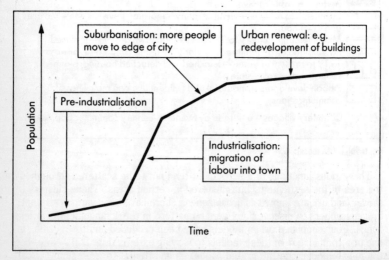

Fig. U.10 Four stages in the development of a settlement

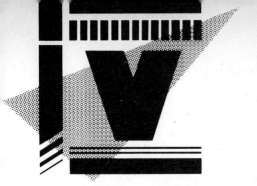

VOLCANOES

Molten lava ejected through a vent in the Earth's crust can solidify close to the vent and build up a conical hill or mountain. Whether this happens, and the final shape of the cone built, depends largely on the nature of the ejected lava. Viscous or acid lava, which does not flow far from the vent before solidifying, develops a steep-sided cone. Basic lava, on the other hand, is 'runny' in texture and flows further before solidifying; a low cone or shield volcano results. Mauna Loa, Hawaii (Fig. V.1), is an example.

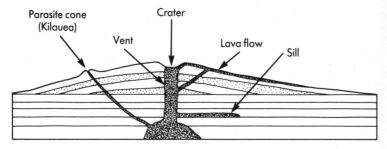

Fig. V.1 Mauna Loa, a symmetrical shield volcano

Many different materials can be ejected during a volcanic eruption; gases, dust, ash, cinders, steam and 'bombs' (solid pieces of rock). Fig. V.2 is a newspaper account of the eruption of Mount St Helens in the USA in 1980.

It is interesting that despite the hazards and dangers of such eruptions, people continue to live close to active volcanic cones. Soils are highly fertile in volcanic areas. Volcanic activity brings other benefits to people (e.g., geothermal energy). Iceland and New Zealand have plentiful supplies of cheap energy. Volcanic areas can also be tourist attractions.

During May 1980 Mount St.Helens, a volcano in Washington State, USA, erupted violently after having been dormant since 1857. The once 3,122-metre mountain lies roughly in the centre of a 300-kilometre-long chain of active volcanoes – the only ones in North America – running south from British Columbia, Canada, to the northern borders of California. The eruption gave little warning, killing some 100 people and leaving behind a trail of disasters.

Here is an account made by a geologist who witnessed the eruption: Heavy, thick, white and blue clouds of pungent gas quickly built up so that the whole area went pitch black. Within seconds the crater's north wall collapsed as a six-cubic-kilometre mass of volcanic dust and rock was blasted up by an explosion 500 times more powerful than the atomic bomb dropped on Hiroshima by the Americans in 1945. Snow was instantly melted and avalanches of mud and rock hurtled down the volcano's slopes at up to 140 km.p.h. Then the cloud of ash, sometimes as hot as 100°C, which had risen 15 kilometres, began to fall over the whole U.S. north west, even on areas over 140 kilometres away.

The once-admired perfect symmetry of the cone was destroyed by the explosion, which blew away the top 500 metres of the mountain to form a four-kilometre-wide, 2,000-metre-deep crater. One week after the eruption the fourth unpleasant expulsion from an erupting volcano – molten lava flowing down the mountain side – had not yet appeared.

Fig. V.2 Newspaper account of the eruption of Mount St Helens.

WATER CYCLE (HYDROLOGICAL)

The world's water supply is contained in a system known as the water cycle (Fig. W.1). Water moves through this system as either a liquid or a vapour (Fig W.2). For instance, there is evaporation, that is, water turning into

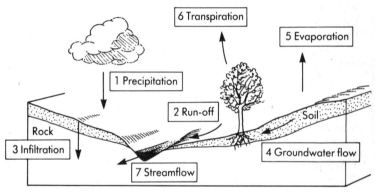

Fig. W.1 The water cycle

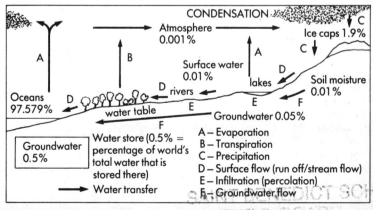

Fig. W.2 The world's water store

water vapour, from seas and rivers and vapour-carrying clouds condense, that is, vapour turning back to water, to produce rain, some of which 'runs off' the Earth's surface and back into rivers and seas.

WATERFALL

A waterfall is a sudden fall of water in the course of a river, usually the result of the presence of a band of hard rock with greater resistance to **erosion** by the running water in the bed of the river (Figs. W.3 and W.4). The water erodes the softer rock around the harder band, leading to the formation of a fall (e.g., Niagara Falls, between Lakes Erie and Ontario in the USA).

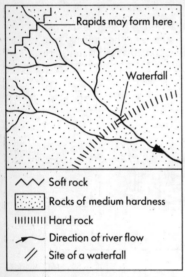

Rapids may form here

Waterfall

∧∧∨ Soft rock

Rocks of medium hardness

|||||||||| Hard rock

Direction of river flow

// Site of a waterfall

Fig. W.3 Formation of waterfalls and rapids

River

Cap rock (hard rock)

Undercutting

Plunge pool

Softer rock

River

Waterfall slowly eroded backwards

Fig. W.4 Waterfall erosion

WATERSHEDS

◀ Drainage basins ▶

WATER TABLE

Normally there is a level beneath rock under the Earth's surface which is permanently saturated. This level is known as the water table and the saturated rocks beneath it as the *ground water* or *aquifer* (Fig. W.5). Miners and desert travellers know about underground water!

The position of the water table normally varies during the year (Fig. W.6).

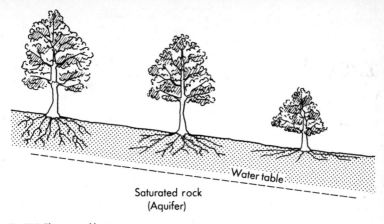

Fig. W.5 The water table

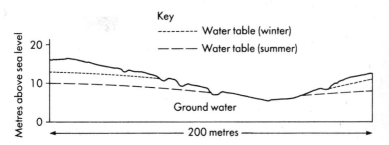

Fig. W.6 Seasonal variation in the water table

The position of the water table normally varies during the year (Fig. W.4). After heavy rainfall and during most winters it rises, but it falls during periods of drought and most summers. Flooding occurs when the depth of the water table has a negative value, in other words, when water which should be below the ground is in fact above it.

WAVE

Waves are the sea's agents of **erosion** and **deposition** which continuously amend coastlines. They are produced by the pressure of the wind making the surface of the sea undulate; the height and power of the waves depends on the strength of the wind and on their fetch, the distance they have been blown across the sea. The forward movement of a wave up a beach is called the swash, its backward or return flow the backwash (Fig. W.7). Fig. W.8 shows the parts of a wave.

The relative strengths of the swash and the backwash determine whether a wave is constructive (deposition exceeds erosion) or destructive (erosion

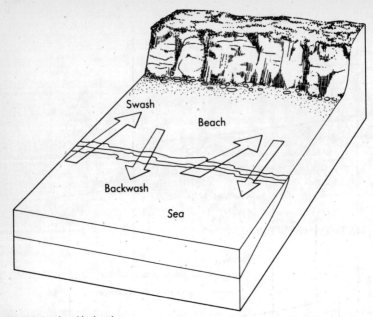

Fig. W.7 Swash and backwash

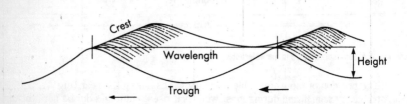

Fig. W.8 Parts of a wave

exceeds deposition). Constructive waves will have a stronger swash, and this is more likely with a lower frequency of arrival (say, six to eight per minute), a longer wavelength and low height. Constructive waves which deposit material on a shoreline are generally shallower and are common on flatter, large beaches. Destructive waves, on the other hand, have a stronger backwash and a higher frequency of arrival (e.g., say, twelve to twenty per minute). They are steep waves and common on steeper beaches. The two types of wave are also known as spilling or surging breakers (constructive) and plunging or surfing breakers (destructive) (Fig. W.9).

◀ Sea defences ▶

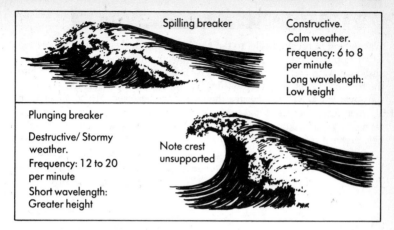

Fig. W.9 Constructive and destructive breakers

WAVE-CUT PLATFORM

This is an erosional feature cut by the waves as part of the general recession (backwards erosion) of a cliffed coastline. The cliff face recedes through undercutting by the sea at the base of the cliff, followed by collapse of the cliff face above. The retreat of the cliff face leaves the old base of the cliff as a platform (Fig. W.10).

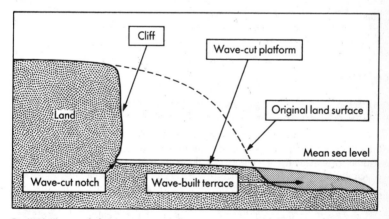

Fig. W.10 Wave cut platform

The waves eroding the coastline carry some of the small rock fragments back out to sea. In time, **deposition** of these fragments may build up to form a terrace, referred to as a wave-built terrace.

WAVE REFRACTION

Waves tend to break parallel to the shoreline, where their motion is checked by friction with the sea bed, but at the points where headlands occur, the shallower water retards wave advance. The rest of the wave moves on into the bay and is bent or refracted (Fig. W.11). This concentrates the energy of the advancing wave front against the side of the headlands. Headland erosion is, therefore, increased by this wave refraction. Long-term, there is a tendency for a coastline of headlands and bays to be smoothed out with the help of wave refraction.

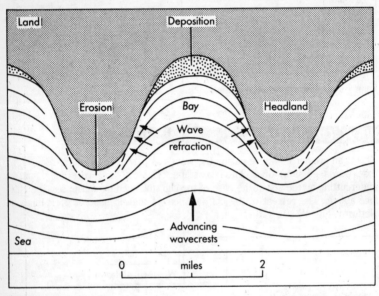

Fig. W.11 Refracted waves

WEATHER AND CLIMATE

There is an important distinction to be drawn between these two terms. Weather refers to the atmospheric conditions at any location for a short period of time. It is made up of a number of elements (e.g., temperature, sunshine, **precipitation**, etc.). The essence of weather is *change*. Weather conditions can change hour by hour, day by day, etc. In Britain, variations in the weather are considerable.

The *climate* is deduced from observations of the weather. It exists as averages in tables and charts, created by people. Weather actually *occurs*; climate is *derived from it*, so that people can get some idea of the general atmospheric conditions which 'normally' exist at a place.

It is often said that Britain has 'no climate, only weather'. Because conditions are changeable and unpredictable in Britain, the climatic averages are not regularly experienced. Places with more predictable weather can be said to have a climate (e.g., summers are reliably hot and dry in Mediterranean countries).

WEATHERING

The term weathering is used to describe the breakdown of rock through exposure to the atmosphere. Rain, wind, heat, frost, temperature change and organisms such as worms are responsible for rock decay and disintegration. The principal difference between **erosion** and weathering is that there is no movement of the broken-down material in the case of weathering. Weathering factors are not, unlike erosional agents, capable of transport. Rock is weathered to provide rock fragments from which soil is formed.

Weathering factors are generally classified into three groups of process: *mechanical* processes such as freeze-thaw, which shatters jointed rocks when water in the joints freezes and expands; *chemical* processes such as hydrolysis, when a chemical reaction between water and a rock mineral leads to the breakdown of the rock; and *biological* processes such as animal burrowing, tree roots embedding themselves in rocks, the decay of dead

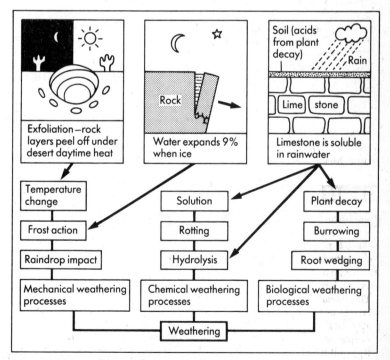

Fig. W.12 Different ways of rock weathering

organisms producing acids, etc. Some of the principal ways in which rock is weathered are shown in Fig. W.12.

Weathering is clearly influenced by climate. In tropical areas, with high temperature and heavy rainfall, chemical weathering is at its maximum. In temperate regions such as Britain both mechanical and chemical weathering are common as a result of frost action, heat expansion of rock and moderate rainfall. In arid areas weathering is mainly mechanical, due to heat during the day and frost at night. In Polar regions there is very little weathering. Taken overall, chemical weathering is the dominant means of rock breakdown in the world today. Hydrolysis is the most important chemical weathering process, and takes place wherever rock and water are in contact.

◄ Deposition ►

WIND

Wind is the air in movement. Both the speed and direction of a wind can be measured, using an anemometer and a wind vane respectively. Winds are named according to the direction of their source. For example, the westerlies, which are the prevailing/predominant winds over the British Isles, blow from the west and bring to this country the weather conditions of the west.

Winds are generated by atmospheric pressure differences, blowing towards low pressure. However, they do not blow across the isobars (lines drawn through places having equal values of atmospheric pressure) down the pressure gradient towards the lower pressure, but rather go nearly along/parallel to the isobars in a curved path towards the lower pressure. This curvature or bending of winds is the result of the Earth's rotation, the deflecting force being known as the Coriolis Force. Winds are deflected to the right in the Northern Hemisphere and to the left in the Southern Hemisphere.

The Coriolis Force changes only the direction of a wind, not its speed. Wind speeds are determined by the spacing of the isobars, that is, the steepness of the pressure gradient. Closely packed isobars lead to strong winds. Wind speeds are measured on the Beaufort Scale, from zero to 12: breezes run from 2 to 6, gales from 7 to 10, storms are described as 11 and hurricanes as 12.

◄ Air masses, General circulation ►

WIND ROSE

A diagram to show, by the length of the directional bars, the frequency of winds blowing from each of the leading points of the compass (Fig. W.13).

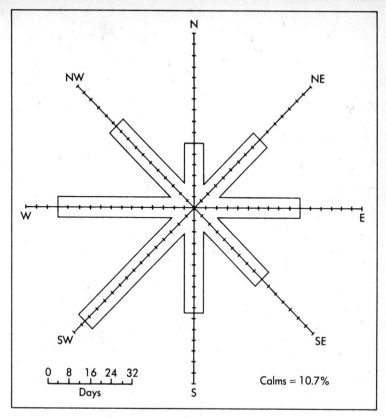

Fig. W.13 A wind rose